NATIONAL HUMAN RIGHTS COMMSSION: AN ASSESSMENT

NATIONAL HUMAN RIGHTS COMMISSION: AN ASSESSMENT
(A Study of its Working from 1994 to 1999)

by

Pinki Gautam

GYAN

The Publication of this thesis was financially upheld by ICSSR and the responsibility of the facts stated, opinions expressed or conclusions reached are entirely that of the author and ICSSR accepts no responsibility for them.

ICSSR Consultant

Prof. B.K. Tewari, Head Political Science, Lucknow University, 302, Tirath Bakshi Apartments (New Hyderabad). Lucknow (U.P.)

ISBN: 978-81-212-1253-3

First Published, 2015

Published by

Gyan Publishing House
5, Ansari Road Daryaganj,
New Delhi-110002
Phones: 9811692060
Fax : 91-11-23285914
E-mail: books@gyanbooks.com

Laser Typesetting: Gyan Print, Delhi
Printed at: G. Print Process, Delhi

Cataloging in Publication Data—DK
Courtesy: D.K. Agencies (P) Ltd. <docinfo@dkagencies.com>

Gautam, Pinki, author.

National Human Rights Commission: An Assessment (A Study of its Working from 1994 to 1999) by Pinki Gautam.

pages ; cm

Originally presented as the author's thesis (Ph. D.) to Dr B.R. Ambedkar University.

Under the Supervision of MS Dr Kanan Gahrana, Reader, Deptt of Political Science, DS College, Aligarh, 2008

Includes bibliographical references and index.

1. India National Human Rights Commission—History. 2. Human rights—India—History. I. Title.

DDC 323.0954 23

Contents

Preface

Human Rights are now universally acknowledged as essential norms of democratic governance. How much a state is politically advanced and progressive, is judged by the status of human rights in that state. The promotion and protection of human rights is considered the solemn duty of the part of the state. Ironically, the state also happens to be the most common violator or usurper of these rights in most of the cases. Hence, there is need to device a mechanism which can ensure the protection of human rights and to act as a watch-dog to discipline the erring behaviour of the state. It is not an easy task. The states are always reluctant to place themselves to any scrutiny and monitoring of their behaviour, more so in the matter of human rights abuses where the needle of suspicion is always pointed at them. It is for this reason that very few states have adopted such national mechanism for enforcing human rights.

India, too, was initially reluctant to the idea of a human rights monitoring system in the guise of a national institution / commission for protecting human rights. However, the continued pressure at the national and international levels and Human Rights NGOs cry against the human rights abuses by the security forces in the wake of anti-insurgency operations and suppression of militancy in Punjab, Jammu and Kashmir and the North-eastern states in 1980s and early 1990s made the government hard pressed to satisfy the human rights protagonists who were demanding a National Human Rights Commission for India. Finally, the Indian Parliament enacted a law known as the Protection of Human Rights Act, 1993 which led to the establishment of the National Human Rights Commission in 1994.

The purpose of this study is to examine the role of NHRC in the protection and promotion of human rights during the first five years of its existence, i.e., from 1994-1999, so as to evaluate how it has played its role as a human rights watch-dog in protecting and promoting human rights and also to suggest what is missing in its functioning and how it can be made more effective in enforcing human rights.

Chapter I discusses the human rights implementation systems operating at international, regional and national levels and brings out the complementary nature of these systems to point out the significance of national human rights systems in enforcing universal human rights norms and standards. Chapter II traces the evolution of the concept of national human rights institutions at the international level and the emergence of the NHRIs in other parts of the world as a background to the making of the NHRC in India. Chapter III deals with the organisation, powers and functions of the NHRC as per the Protection of Human Rights Act, 1993 and its actual functioning. Chapters IV and V evaluate the role of the NHRC in the protection and promotion of human rights. Lastly, Chapter VI brings out the concluding observations on the working and performance of the NHRC in the first five years of its inception.

First of all, I am immensely grateful to my supervisor, Dr (Ms) Kanan Gahrana, Reader in the Department of Political Science at D.S. College, Aligarh who introduced me to the world of human rights studies and without whose able guidance and constant encouragement I could not achieve my goal. She has been extremely patient with me at the most provocative moments. I am thankful to her for bearing with me and my problems.

I am also thankful to the Indian Council of Social Science Research, New Delhi for awarding me a short-term research fellowship to enable me to meet the necessary expenses related with this project. The financial help extended by this fellowship has contributed in enhancing the quality of this work. In this regard, I would like to express my gratitude to Shri O.P. Sharma of the ICSSR for his kind help.

My thanks are also due to my teachers at the Department of Political Science, D.S. College, Aligarh, namely, Dr Y.C. Nigam, Dr D.K. Gaur and Dr (Ms) Madhu Varshney who all have always been very encouraging to me and were always ready to help me.

I would like to express my thanks to the librarians and their staff at various libraries that I consulted during the course of this research work. These include Parliament Library, New Delhi, Nehru Memorial Library, New Delhi, Library of the Ministry of Home Affairs, Govt of India, New Delhi, the NHRC Library, New Delhi, Jawaharlal Nehru University Library, New Delhi, the Law Department Library, AMU, Aligarh and the Maulana

Azad Library, AMU, Aligarh. They were all very cooperative to me in my search for the relevant material for this work.

I owe my special gratitude to Ms Kamlesh Jain and Dr Sudha Raghavan of Jawaharlal Nehru University, New Delhi who very kindly extended me all possible hospitality during my stay with them and offered all possible help in exploring the necessary material for this project.

Above all, this venture would not have been possible but for the support and encouragement of my parents and also the cooperation extended by my brothers and sister Montu, Sontu, Rinki and Arti and other family members. I will be failing in my duty if I do not acknowledge the love and patience shown by my little daughter and the whole-hearted cooperation of my dear husband who never complained about the discomfort which they had to face because of my preoccupation with this work. I am also thankful to M/s Mittal Computers, Bhagwati Palace, Samad Road, Aligarh for the neat and careful typing of the manuscript.

Pinki Gautam

Chapter - I

Introduction

Today, we are living in the age of democracy where human rights are in vogue. Human rights are variously referred as natural rights, basic rights and inalienable rights. But strictly speaking, human rights are those rights which all humans possess by virtue of their being borned as humans. These rights belong to them because of their very existence and become operative from the moment of their coming into being. Human rights are essentially those rights which a person requires to lead a dignified human existence. As has been rightly defined, 'human rights are the rights that everyone has, and everyone equally, by virtue of their humanity.'[1]

No doubt, the etymology of the concept of human rights goes back to ancient times; however, the term 'human rights' is of recent coinage.[2] The newness of human rights is not confined to its nomenclature merely, but it extends to its contents and approach as well. Content wise, human rights have evolved to include individual and collective rights in its ambit besides extending its range to cover civil and political rights, economic, social and cultural rights and also the so-called Third Generation rights[3] as well. Approach wise, modern approach to human rights led to making universal appeal and development of institutional framework for the purpose of protection and promotion of human rights.

The movement for the universal recognition of human rights began with the struggle for the democratic rights and freedoms in the West against the medieval feudal regimes. It journeyed through the Magna Carta (1215), the Petition of Rights (1628), the Agreement of the People (1647), the Bill of Rights (1688), the Virginia Declaration of Rights (1776), the French Declaration of the Rights of Man (1789), the Communist

Manifesto (1848) and many more; and finally arriving at the Universal Declaration of Human Rights (1948). As of now, human rights are universally acclaimed as the yardstick of a nation's credibility as a civilised nation in the contemporary international society.

Internationalisation of Human Rights

Before the advent of the United Nations, human rights in general were considered a matter of domestic jurisdiction of sovereign states. It was a matter of sovereign discretion with the states whether to recognise and guarantee protection of human rights or defy them with impunity. In principle, the state of human rights – even in the Nazist Germany – was not the concern of the international system, or of international politics, or of international law. The inclusion of the words 'to promote respect for human rights and fundamental freedoms' in the Dumbarton Oaks proposals in 1944 sowed the seeds of the international human rights movement.[4]

The principle of international concern for human rights found expression in the Charter of the United Nations – the first international instrument which, in unequivocal terms, proclaimed 'universal respect for, and observance of, human rights and fundamental freedom for all without distinction as to race, sex, language or religion.' The Charter made promotion of these rights as one of the basic purposes of the United Nations and obligated member States' to take joint and separate action in cooperation with the United Nations for the achievement of this purpose. It was for the first time in the history of mankind, human rights were being universalised and internationalised – rights which every individual whatever one's origin could claim as a member of human society.[5]

The Charter of the United Nations refers to the issue of human rights in its Preamble and in six different Articles concerning different organs of the U.N. However, the provision of Article 2, paragraph 7 upholds the principle of non-intervention in the matters of domestic jurisdiction of the states in general, but if it poses threats to the peace, breaches of the peace, and acts of aggression, then enforcement measures are permissible under Chapter VII.[6]

The UN Charter has laid down the general principles relating to the universal nature of human rights, but it does not define or enlist 'human rights and fundamental freedoms.' This task was performed by the General Assembly which proclaimed the Universal Declaration of Human Rights in 1948. The Universal Declaration of Human Rights (UDHR hereafter) defines specific rights – civil and political as well as economic, social and cultural – with equality and freedom from discrimination as a principal and recurrent theme. The Universal Declaration of Human Rights is not a legally binding multi-lateral treaty but it is a declaration of intent and an expression of collective opinion of the international community with regard to 'a common standard of achievement' for all people and all nations in respect of human rights. It was the first step in the direction of international norms-setting in human rights. It made an impact in the sense that various provisions of the UDHR have been adopted in national constitutions, other international instruments and regional treaties and conventions as well.

Pursuant to the adoption of the UDHR, efforts were made to prepare draft of international instrument to put into binding legal form the rights proclaimed in the UDHR. After twenty years of prolonged debates, negotiations, compromises and accommodation of divergent viewpoints, two separate International Covenants – one on civil and political rights (ICCPR hereafter) and the other on economic, social and cultural rights – were adopted unanimously by the General Assembly on 16 December, 1966. The ICCPR had an Optional Protocol as well. These instruments, along with the UDHR itself and a second Optional Protocol adopted in 1989, make up what is now widely known as the International Bill of Human Rights.[7]

In addition to the International Bill of Human Rights, the United Nations has developed an impressive body of substantive norms of human rights covering a whole range of human rights. The United Nations keeps on adding new instruments to the catalogue of human rights whenever and wherever the need is felt by the international community for an elaboration of the norms concerning newly emerging human rights issues, e.g., the declaration on the right to development, right to peace, right to a clean and healthy environment and other third generation of human rights.

The international system of human rights is not confined to merely norms-setting on rights and freedoms and on state obligations, but it also includes a system of monitoring and supervision at the international level. It means a mechanism by which international bodies examine the way in which states live upto their obligations in regard to respect for and observance and implementation of human rights.

UN Human Rights Bodies

Besides assigning human rights responsibilities to the principal organs of the United Nations, the Charter has provided for specific bodies to be established under these organs – independent and subsidiary – for the promotion of human rights.

Relying on the mandate, as given by Article 68 of the Charter, Economic and Social Council (ECOSOC hereafter) established several functional commissions. The Commission on Human Rights and the Commission on the Status of Women were two for them which were set up in 1946. A Sub-Commission on Prevention of Discrimination and Protection of Minorities was set up in 1947.

Commission on Human Rights*

*The Commission on Human Rights has been replaced by the UN Human Rights Councils in June 2006 with slight modifications.

The UN Commission on Human Rights is composed of fifty-three members elected for a three year term. It is responsible for submitting proposals, recommendations and investigative reports on human rights issues through ECOSCO to the General Assembly. Over a period of time, the commission has developed to be the prevailing human rights body of the United Nations, offering a forum for States, intergovernmental and non-governmental organisations to speak out their concerns on human rights issues. Located at Geneva, the Commission on Human Rights meets for six weeks in a year. It has set up mechanisms to investigate human rights problems in specific countries and territories as well as on thematic situations. It makes use of working-groups as well as Special Rapporteurs on specific countries and issues for investigative purposes. It has played an important role in norms-setting efforts of the United Nations in respect of human rights issues.[8]

Commission on the Status of Women

The Commission on the Status of Women was established as a special organ to deal with women's issues and work for gender equality. Comprised of forty-five members, it studies women's progress towards equality throughout the world, makes recommendations on promoting women's rights in political, economic, social and educational fields, addresses problems demanding immediate attention in the field of women's rights. It also prepares draft-treaties and other instruments aimed at improving the status of women in law and in practice.

The commission's activities have evolved from defining rights to examining factors that have prevented women from enjoying them. It has also contributed in establishing a firm base in international law of the norms of equality. It is also responsible for promoting an international women's rights movement. Women's rights are integral to human rights. Thus, the Commission on the Status of Women is an integral part of the human rights machinery of the United Nations.[9]

Sub-commission on the Prevention of Discrimination and the Protection of Minorities

The Sub-commission on the Prevention of Discrimination and the Protection of Minorities was set-up by the ECOSOC in 1947 to aid the Commission on Human Rights in its tasks. It consists of twenty six experts from all regions of the world. It makes recommendations and conducts investigations on issues dealing with the prevention of discrimination and protection of ethnic, religious, racial and linguistic minorities.[10]

Centre for Human Rights

The Centre for Human Rights, situated in Geneva, was established to assist the organs of the United Nations in the promotion and protection of human rights, to undertake research / studies at the request of the organs concerned, and to publish and disseminate information on human rights. The centre also serves various human rights bodies including the Commission on Human Rights and the Sub-commission on the Prevention of Discrimination and the Protection of Minorities.

It comprises the office of the Assistant Secretary-General for Human Rights and the office of the High-Commissioner on Human Rights as well. The working of the centre is well-organised under the five branches. The Communication Branch processes communications concerning alleged human rights violations. The Special Procedures Branch provides necessary services to the investigative organs set up by human rights bodies, such as working groups and special rapporteurs, and organises field missions. The International Instruments Branch follows the implementation of human rights treaties and conventions. The Legislation and Prevention of Discrimination Branch assists in preparing international human rights instruments and prepares studies and reports requested by the Sub-commission. The Technical and Advisory Services Branch administers the programme of advisory services and technical assistance, including the Voluntary Funds for Technical Cooperation and Advisory Services. The centre has field-offices in several countries, e.g., Burundi, Cambodia, Crotia, Guatemala, Malawi & Rwanda.[11]

High Commissioner for Human Rights

The post of the United Nations High Commissioner for Human Rights was created in December 1993 by the General Assembly following the recommendation made by the Vienna Declaration on Human Rights.[12] The High Commissioner for Human Rights is the principal official responsible for the over all United Nations Human Rights activities who functions under the direction and authority of the Secretary General.

The High Commissioner's tasks include coordination of different human rights activities under the United Nations system; rationalising, adapting, strengthening and streamlining the United Nations machinery to improve its efficiency and effectiveness; and supervising the working of the Centre for Human Rights. The High Commissioner is also responsible for enhancing international cooperation for the promotion and protection of human rights.[13]

International Human Rights Implementation Mechanisms

Over a period of time, the United Nations has evolved various mechanism to implement the international norms relating to human rights. These mechanisms relate to monitoring system, complaint system, enforcement and prosecution measures.

The UN Commission on Human Rights and its Sub-Commission on Prevention of Discrimination and Protection of Minorities monitor the human rights situation around the world. They discuss violations of human rights wherever they occur in their meetings which remain open to the press and public. They examine the facts presented by the governments involved as well as the non-governmental organisations. If required, they make use of their own fact-finding groups or expert-groups, undertake on-the-spot visits to find the facts themselves. On the basis of the facts gathered, they first persuade the concerned government to take necessary measures needed to restore full enjoyment of human rights, provide assistance if desired and condemn the violations in case of failure. The Commission also studies human rights as a global phenomenon by investigating 'thematic' human rights issues and violations which are not specific to a particular country. For this purpose, mechanisms such as the working group or Special Rapporteurs are adopted.[14]

ECOSOC and all the UN human rights treaty bodies, including the Human Rights Committee (under the Optional Protocol to the ICCPR), receive reports from various countries regarding the state of human rights, study them and make comments and recommendations thereupon as may be appropriate. The reporting procedure, as it is known, is the most common international procedure of implementation. Regarding other mechanisms such as interstate complaint procedure, there are isolated instances of the use of this procedure as states generally prefer to take a human rights dispute to a forum where they have greater political clout, such as the UN Human Rights Commission or the Security Council or the General Assembly. [15]

The complaints which fall outside the treaty-based complaint mechanism are handled under the 1503 procedure. This procedure is governed mainly by ECOSOC resolution 1503 (XL VIII) of 27 May, 1970. Under this procedure, any individual can complaint against any country even if it is not a Member of the United Nations. These complaints are directly sent to the Secretary General who refers them to the Commission on Human Rights and Sub-Commission on Prevention of Discriminations and Protection of Minorities. Complaints are discussed in closed meetings and remain confidential until the commission decides to submit a report to ECOSOC.[16]

It has been observed that complaints of human rights violations stand better chance of redressal if they are addressed to human rights treaty bodies like the Human Rights Committee, the Committee Against Torture (CAT), or the Committee on the Elimination of Racial Discrimination (CERD), etc. These bodies consider individual complaints falling within their respective jurisdiction and grant remedies to those found to have suffered violations of their human rights.[17] Thus, the complaint redressal mechanism of human rights treaty-based bodies is more effective in protection of human rights compared to the 1503 procedure.

As far as the enforcement mechanisms are concerned, the Security Council is the only UN organ capable of and responsible for taking enforcement measures. Promotion of respect for human rights is collective responsibility of the UN system as a whole, including the Security Council. Conversely, the Security Council is required to act in accordance with the purposes and principles of the United Nations. Although, the

Security Council is not directly responsible for the protection of human rights; however, it has been entrusted with the primary responsibility to maintain international peace and security for which it is empowered to take appropriate measures, including measures aimed at the pacific settlement of disputes and enforcement action as well. In situations where gross violations of human rights lead to a threat to international peace and security, the Security Council can take appropriate action and it has taken action on several such occasions in the past.[18] Yet, the Security Council is not the right forum for handling human rights issues as its highly political functioning mars the very spirit of human rights philosophy.

No doubt, the United Nations has evolved a large number of implementation mechanisms for the protection of human rights and its efforts relating to norms-setting and institution-building are equally commendable, but in terms of its effectiveness, the international system of implementation of human rights suffers from inherent weaknesses. The biggest weakness of the international system is the principle of national sovereignty which creates obstacles in ensuring international accountability, and cultural diversity prevails over the universality of human rights. The functioning of the United Nations is predominantly guided by national interests of dominant powers who are more inclined to indulge in the politics of human rights instead of engaging themselves with the promotion of universal human rights.

Moreover, international human rights implementation mechanisms under the UN system are marred by several shortcomings. The late submission of status-reports by the Member-states, poor-quality of these reports, procedural delays and lethargic follow-up actions plague the reporting system. Further, interstate complaint procedures being an optional mechanism, not many states have opted for it. Similarly, individual petition procedures too are optional. The 1503 procedure of the ECOSOC rarely produces tangible outcome. The Security Council, owing to its veto system, also does not find it easy to enforce action against human rights violators. As a whole, international human rights implementation system has its own constraints and restraints resulting in an ineffective and weak implementation of human rights globally.

Regional Human Rights Systems

The task of promoting and protecting human rights is not one which could or should be assumed by only one organisation. The international system relies heavily on the support it receives from regional human rights systems such as the ones functional in Europe, Latin – America and Africa. Regional human rights systems play an important complementary role in reinforcing international standards and machinery by providing the means by which human rights concern can be addressed within particular social, historical and political context of the region concerned.[19]

As of now, there are three regional human rights systems in place, with their own permanent institutions functioning for the protection and promotion of human rights. They are : the European human rights system, the Inter-American human rights system, and the African human rights system. But, there is no regional human rights system for Asia.

European Human Rights System

The European human rights system is the oldest of all regional human rights systems and is also the most effective and mature regional system. Taking its clue from the adoption of the Universal Declaration on Human Rights (UDHR) by the United Nations in 1948, the Council of Europe adopted the European Convention on Human Rights in 1950 which entered into force in 1953.[20] All member-states of the Council of Europe are party to the convention and have recognised the right to individual petition under Article 25 of the Convention, with the exception of Cyprus, Greece, Malta and Turkey who have not given specific declaration to this effect.

There are six additional protocols to the convention providing for the extension of the rights guaranteed by the convention, procedural amendments and empowering the court with advisory jurisdiction. In addition to these ratified additional protocols, two more protocols have also been opened for signature; one of which deals with the acceleration of the procedure before the European Court of Human Rights.[21]

Under the European system, the task of implementation of human rights is entrusted to three controlling organs which include the European Commission of Human Rights, the European Court of Human Rights, and the Committee of Ministers of the Council of Europe. The implementation system provides for both inter-state complaints and individual complaints. The latter is rather more efficient than the former.

The European Commission of Human Rights is the primary institution entrusted with the responsibility to handle the complaints of human rights violations. It is a quasi-judicial body consisting of the number of independent experts equal to the number of states that are party to the convention. These members are elected by the Committee of Ministers and function in their individual capacity. The first stage relates to the examination of the complaints from the point of view of their admissibility. There are a number of criteria which have to be met, including proof by the applicant that all effective remedies available under the domestic jurisdiction have been exhausted; the complaint may not be anonymous and must not be manifestly ill-founded.[22] Once a complaint is admitted, the commission goes on to establish the facts and then to try if possible to secure a friendly settlement.

In case of failure to reach a settlement, the commission sends a report to the government and the Committee of Ministers. The government or the Committee of Ministers may also refer the case to the European Court of Human Rights. However, the 9th Protocol to the Convention allows individual applicants to take the case to the Court, provided that the country of which he / she is a citizen has signed the Protocol. The Court proceedings are public and judgements which are final are delivered in a public sessions.

Over the years, the European Court of Human Rights has delivered judgements on a very wide range of issues and its decisions are binding upon the country concerned. Hence, the European system has effectively influenced national legislation as well as put up a formidable body of jurisprudence relating to the interpretation of the rights under the convention.[23]

However, the role of the Committee of Ministers in resoltuion of the cases referred to it is not devoid of criticisms. The procedure followed in the committee is not public. Its decisions are not exclusively based on legal merits which is quite natural since it is basically a political organ. The Committee of Ministers is entrusted with two tasks, namely, consideration of complaints which have not been referred to the European Court of Human Rights and supervising the execution of the judgement of the Court.[24] A two-thirds majority is required to find a violation at the committee level where as the court operates by simple majority.

There is also a provision for reporting procedure under Article 57 of the convention, but it is not every effective. The sporadic use of this provision weakens the importance of monitoring mechanisms.

The European Convention on Human Rights is devoted exclusively to political and civil rights. Economic, social and cultural rights are espoused by the European Social Charter which came into force in 1965.

The implementation mechanism under the charter requires the state parties to submit a country status report with regard to the charter's provisions to the Secretary-General of the Council of Europe every two years. These reports are examined by a Committee of Independent Experts who forward it to a Committee of Government Representatives with their expert comments. Further, it is forwarded to the Parliamentary Assembly which finally passes its conclusions and views on to the Committee of Ministers which may make recommendations to each of the state parties. This entire procedure is not very satisfying as it involves major political / diplomatic interplay of governments. However, the real contribution has been made by the Committee of Experts who have built up a vast body of 'case-law' on the European interpretation of social rights.[25]

A positive advance of the European human rights system is seen in the implementation mechanism of the European Convention for the Prevention of Torture and Inhuman or Degrading Treatment or Punishment which came into force in 1987. An innovative aspect of this convention is the machinery of a preventive nature which provides for impromptu visits by the committee of ten independent experts to all places of detention in the territories of state-parties to the convention. Their findings are not made public but are conveyed to the government in each case. This is a positive advance as for the most part, even where machinery exists, to combat torture the control mechanism tends to be of a reactive nature.[26]

Other positive features of the European system include : awarding 'just satisfaction' and *restitutio in integrum* by the court and giving free legal aid to the applicant during the procedures of the commission. Furthermore, the European system has handled inter-state cases successfully. One of them even became subject of a judgement by the European Court of Human Rights. This category of complaints has not usually occurred in other international systems.[27]

Inter-American Human Rights System

The Inter-American Human Rights System has evolved through various stages finding its roots in the Charter of the Organisation of American States (OAS thereafter) and the American Declaration of the Rights and Duties of Man in 1948. In 1959, the OAS started working on the draft of a regional human rights treaty which finally got adopted in 1978 as the American Convention of Human Rights, resulting in the modification of institutional and legal framework of the inter-American human rights system.

In the interim period, the OAS had established the Inter-American Commission on Human Rights in 1959, by a political resolution, not by a treaty. It's main purpose was to study the human rights situation in the Member-States of the OAS. The commission was authorised to hold meetings in the countries it visited and prepare Country-Reports. These reports were sent to the concerned governments to seek their observations and then made public and submitted to the OAS General Assembly for its consideration. By 1965, the commission was given the authority to handle individual petitions.[28]

Before the adoption of the American Convention on Human Rights, the American commission was an 'autonomous entity' whose main function was to promote the observance and protection of human rights and to serve as a consultative organ of the OAS in the field of human rights. But, the status of the commission has changed under the American Convention on Human Rights. Now, it is one of the principal organs of the OAS. Another change that has been effected by the American convention is the creation of two categories of members. The convention distinguishes between 'member-states' (the OAS Member-States) and 'states-parties' (state-parties to the convention) in defining the functions of the Commission. According to the convention, the human rights contained in the American conventions are applicable on the states parties whereas in relation to the member-states, the provisions contained in the American Declaration of Rights and Duties of Man are applicable. The commission carries out its functions, keeping this distinction of membership in mind.[29]

The procedure for handling individual petitions is similar to that of the European system and the Optional Protocol to the ICCPR. But it has some significant differences which reflect the political and social background against which the system operates. As a number of states in the region are ruled by military-junta or do not observe Rule of Law, the adapted procedure under the Article 46 of the convention allows the admissibility provision requiring 'exhaustion of domestic remedies' to be waived in the case of individuals who cannot do so given the political system of their country. The grounds of admissibility of petition seem very flexible here as there is no restriction of nationality of the complainant. However, the negative aspect is that there is no free legal aid available for the complainants as seen in the European system.[30]

The occurrence of inter-state complaints does not seem very probable due to the small number of states which have given the declaration accepting the jurisdiction in this regard. The system of inter-state complaints was an invention of the convention, although this possibility was not specifically excluded in the pre-convention period. In fact, the commission was requested by the governments of Honduras and El Salvador to investigate the complaints submitted by them against each other in 1969.[31]

In addition, the Inter-American Commission has many sided investigatory, conciliatory and reporting powers, enabling both written and oral stages of work. Furthermore, the achieved friendly settlement is made public as in the European system. The inter-American bodies also have special measures to deal with urgent cases.[32]

Another important institution under the convention is the Inter-American Court of Human Rights. It is not an organ of the inter-American system as the commission is. Its legal foundation is based on the American Convention of Human Rights. So, only the states parties to the convention and the commission may refer a case to the Court, and not individuals. The court's competence as a decision-making body is not automatically derived from the convention. There has to be a declaration to a state party which can be made at any time, unconditionally, but subject to reciprocity, for a specified period or for specific cases. But its competence as a consultative body regarding the convention or some other treaties results directly from the convention. The judgements of the court are final and they are not subject to appeal. The states parties to the convention agree to comply with the judgements in cases in which they are involved.[33]

Though, the inter-American system is inspired by the European Convention on Human Rights, but its judicial foundation is not as solid as that of the European system. Non-ratification of the American Convention of Human Rights by the half of member-states of the OAS resulting in the dual functions of the commission and limited jurisdiction of the court, all this adversely affects the efficiency of the system.

African Human Rights System

One more regional human rights system is operating in the framework of the Organisation of African Unity (OAU hereafter). The charter of the OAU reaffirms the principles of the UN Charter and the Universal Declaration of Human Rights and also mentions the right to self-determination, freedom from colonial rule and the welfare and well-being of African people.

In 1981, the OAU conference of the heads of states and governments adopted the African Charter on Human and Peoples' Rights (the Banjul Charter) at Nairobi. It came into force in 1986. This charter includes both the individual and collective rights. It has been ratified by 40 states parties to the OAU.[34]

In 1987, the African Commission on Human and Peoples' Rights was established by the Banjul Charter. The OAU member-states were not very inclined to make the African Commission a really effective body particularly in the matter of protection of human rights. They were keen to see it more as a body meant for the promotion of human rights. The charter is not very clear about the powers of the commission with regard to petitions and on enforcing its findings. While this vagueness offered the commission an opportunity to define itself, it also placed profound limitations on the range of possible action.[35]

The African Commission on Human and People's Rights is composed of eleven members who are first nominated by states parties and elected by the Assembly of Heads of State and Government of the OAU, which is also responsible for funding the commission. The commission is a quasi-judicial body with independent status endorsed by its rules of procedures and its members are independent experts who discharge their duties impartially. Participation of non-governmental organisations is permitted at its sessions and observer status is granted to some of these organisations.

The African Commission's mandate consists of both promotional and protective functions. Promotional activities include dissemination of information, research on issues concerning Africans' human rights, publication, teaching and human rights training; also, quasi-legislative activity related to encouraging states to ratify the charter as well as other international human rights instruments and to introduce domestic legislation in order to ensure compliance with its obligations under the charter.

The protective system under the African Commission comprises periodic state reporting mechanism similar to the procedure followed by the UN Human Rights Committee under the ICCPR; inter-state petition procedure dealing with complaints of human rights violations within the purview of the charter; and petitions from individuals and organisations alleging violation of rights. In the case of individual/organisation sent petitions, admissibility criteria must be complied with. Communications from victims alleging violation by a state party can originate not only from the victim himself / herself but also from some one on his / her behalf. The rules of procedure govern how the commission would go about to publish its report in the case of states' complaints where no resolution is arrived at. Or, in the case of individual communications, to undertake an in-depth study of the subject of the situation.[36]

The absence of a court in the African human rights system makes it less effective as adjudicator in cases of complaints of human rights violations. The African complaint system reflects a strong preference for mediation, conciliation and consensus in contrast to confrontational or adversial procedures. Confidentiality until OAU Assembly of Heads of State and Government decides otherwise is also central.

In the initial period, the African Commission lacked the confidence to assert its authority as it had not even resolved the question whether it was mandated to 'decide' on cases, or merely make recommendations to the OAU. But, of late, the African Commission has become more responsive and active towards reported cases of human rights violations and has adopted innovative procedures to investigate and examine the human rights issues of the African region. The commission has taken decisive action on communications against Nigeria, Cameroon, Malawi and Burundi. Special Rapporteur was appointed to study the problem of extra-judicial executions in Africa. In 1996, it appointed another Special Rapporteur on prisons and conditions of detention in Africa. It undertook its first ever on-site missions to Mauritania and Senegal based on a flexible interpretation of the somewhat restrictive charter.[37] Thus, the African Commission is still in its infancy struggling to stand firm on the ground and assert its authority for the protection and promotion of human rights in Africa which is the most trouble-torn region in the world.

From the point of view of implementation of human rights, regional systems have proven more effective than the international human rights system. The complaint systems of international bodies have varied mechanisms and are, therefore, more complicated in contrast to regional systems with less variation. Secondly, the regional systems are basically concerned with the protection of human rights (with the exception of the Inter-American Commission) whereas the main concern of the international system is the promotional activities in the field of human rights; dealing with complaints constitutes a minor task among other things for international bodies. Thirdly, the accessibility of NGOs to international bodies with complaints is limited to those bodies only or to that system only which is not based on convention; whereas in the regional systems which are mainly based on conventions, NGOs have easy access to them. Fourthly, the occurrence of inter-state cases in the regional systems is a very distinctive feature in addition to the measures which can be taken by Courts of Human Rights which do not exist at all in international system. In international system, there is great reluctance to refer the disputes to the International Court of Justice while in the regional systems even special courts have been set up for the purpose. Fifthly, in the international system, there is little eagerness to establish special conciliation commissions; whereas in the regional systems the permanent bodies such as the Commissions on Human Rights, automatically aim at friendly settlement. Sixthly, the decisions under the regional systems are comparatively more binding in nature in contrast to the international system which have to content itself with giving recommendations or striving at friendly settlements. Seventhly, in the matter of use of sanctions, both the international and regional systems avoid taking recourse to them as the ultimate option. However, the action taken against Greece by the Council of Europe almost amounted to expulsion; whereas international human rights bodies themselves do not always have sanctions at their disposal and systems based on conventions do not include any kind of sanctions at all. Eighthly, in the international system, there is often a total lack of follow-up methods whereas they are present in regional systems. Lastly, there is no provision for free legal aid in the international system as is the case in the European system.[38]

Hence, regional systems appear better equipped to handle the problems of human rights violations and work for the protection of human rights. It certainly does not mean that international system has no significant role to play in it. In fact, international system has inspired the regional systems and continues to set the goals for regional and national institutions.

National Human Rights System

The United Nations has taken a lead in the universalisation of human rights by setting universal human rights norms and standards, evolving monitoring mechanisms, promoting compliance and investigating violations of human rights. But without the additional support at regional and national levels, the realisation of human rights is practically not possible.

Like the regional systems, the role of national governments in the realisation of human rights is equally, and in fact more important. Human rights are intimately linked with individual and state. The notion of human rights makes sense only in the context of an organised society, with public authorities. Therefore, the practical task of protecting and promoting human rights is primarily a national one, for which each state must be responsible.

At the national level, rights can be best protected through constitutional/legislative guarantees, an independent judiciary, the enactment and enforcement of individual safeguards and remedies, and the establishment and strengthening of democratic institutions. Activities aimed at the promotion of human rights and cultivation and nurturing of human rights culture should also be viewed as primarily national responsibilities.[39]

A national human rights protection system comprises all those structures and institutions of governance which ensure that all persons enjoy all human rights – civil, political, cultural, social and economic. This includes widely represented legislature, independent and impartial judiciary, responsive and responsible executive, free and fearless media, and alert and active civil society. Besides this usual democratic set-up, the effective implementation of human rights also needs the establishment of a specially designed national institution exclusively devoted to the protection and promotion of human rights, and which is independent of the government and given the mandate to investigate complaints of human rights violations against the state machinery as well. Such institutions are known as 'national human rights institutions' (hereafter NHRIs) and they are, now, an important component of national human rights protection system.

However, there is a view which does not support the establishment of the NHRIs as it finds it unnecessary to waste scarce state resources on these bodies which have nothing special to contribute that an independent judiciary and democratically elected parliament cannot ensure in preventing human rights abuses.

Unfortunately, history tells us otherwise. A body that is in some way separated from the responsibilities of executive governance and judicial administration is in a position to take a leading role in the field of human rights. By maintaining its real and perceived distance from the government of the day, such a body can make a unique contribution to a country's efforts to protect its citizens and to develop a culture respectful to human rights and fundamental freedoms.[40]

Moreover, the NHRIs play complementary role in relation to other state institutions and add value to them by sharing their obligations with respect to the protection and promotion of human rights which they may find unable to do. For example, the judicial procedures are very time consuming and costs a lot. Hence, poor people and victims of human rights abuses stand little chance to get justice. Whereas the NHRIs are known for easy accessibility and simplified expeditious functioning. In some contrast to the courts, the NHRIs are free to play pro-active role by resorting to *suo-motu* action and making intervention as an *amicus curiae*. Equipped with other quasi-judicial functions, they are seen as core to national protection systems and effective country engagement through their capacity to assist in implementation of international human rights norms. Considering the important and constructive role being played by the NHRIs in the national human rights protection system, there has been a renewed emphasis on it as evident from the report of the UN Secretary-General:

'The capacity of the United Nations to help individual countries to build strong human rights institutions will be strengthened...Building strong human rights institutions at the country level is what in the long run will ensure that human rights are protected and advanced in a sustained manner. The emplacement or enhancement of a national protection system in each country, reflecting international human rights norms, should therefore be a principal objective of the organisation. These activities are especially important in countries emerging from conflict.'[41]

The significance of the NHRIs is not confined to national limits only. National human rights institutions are here to stay as national, regional and international actors in ensuring respect for human rights. They are key to the establishment of national human right protection systems. The increasing recognition of the importance of international human rights standards, and their further development, and an appreciation of human rights as interdependent, indivisible and interacted, are the background for the future work of national institutions and the strengthening of national protection systems.[42]

Thus, the NHRIs have emerged as the most-effective and alive tools of implementation of international human rights standards and norms at the national level. They represent the synthesis of international and national approaches for the implementation of human rights. The NHRIs are capable of influencing national governments to abide by international human rights standards and ready to contribute substantially to the work of the international and regional human rights systems by participating and passing on their expert knowledge and practical experience in human rights matters. No doubt, investing in the NHRIs can ensure rich human rights dividends.

References

1. R.J. Vincent, *Human Rights and International Relations*, (Cambridge : 1986), p.13.
2. The term 'human rights' was firstly used by President Franklin D. Roosevelt in his famous Four Freedoms speech.
3. The third generation rights include right to development, right to clean and healthy environment, right to peace, etc., which are collective rights in nature.
4. Yogesh K. Tyagi, "Golden Jubilee of an Unfinished Task : The United Nations Human Rights Movement", *International Studies* 32(4), (New Delhi : 1995), pp. 445-446.
5. K.P. Saksena, *Teaching Human Rights : A Manual for Adult Education,* (New Delhi : 1996), p.18.
6. *United Nations Action In the Field of Human Rights*, Twenty-Fifth Anniversary of the Universal Declaration of Human Rights, United Nations, (New York : 1974), p. 6.
7. *Basic Facts About the United Nations*, Department of Public Information, United Nations, (New York : 1995), p.191.
8. *Ibid.*, pp. 193-194.
9. *Ibid.*, p. 204
10. *Ibid.*, p.194
11. *Ibid.*, p.197
12. Vienna Declaration and Programme of Action, Part II, para 18.
13. *Basic Facts About the United Nations*, op. cit, pp. 196-197.
14. *Ibid.*, pp. 197-198.
15. Tyagi, Op.cit., p. 450.
16. *Basic Facts About the United Nations*, op.cit., pp. 199-200.
17. Tyagi, op.cit., p. 451.

18. For example, in Burundi, Haiti, Iraq, Namibia, Rwanda, South Africa and Southern Rhodesia, the Security Council adopted several enforcement measures.
19. *National Human Rights Institutions*, Professional Training, Series No.4, Centre for Human Rights, United Nations : (New York and Geneva : 1995), p.3.
20. A.H. Robertson, "*Human Rights in Europe*" (2nd ed. 1977), pp. 202-03.
21. A. Subbian, "*Human Rights Complaints System : International and Regional*", (New Delhi : 2003), pp. 112-113.
22. The conditions of admissibility of complaints are laid down in Articles 26 and 27 of the European Convention on Human Rights.
23. Leah Levin, "Implementation Mechanisms at Regional and International Levels", in *Human Rights : Perspectives & Challenges in 1990 and Beyond,* (ed.) K.P. Saksena, (New Delhi : 1994), p. 535.
24. These two tasks are assigned by Articles 32 and 54 respectively under the European Convention on Human Rights.
25. Leah Levin, op.cit., p.536.
26. *Ibid.*
27. A. Subbian, op.cit., p.130.
28. Leah Levin, op.cit., p.536.
29. Charter Article 51 raised the Commission to the status of a "Principal Organ", Art. 112 describes the functions of the Organisation, Art. 150 provided for the status of the American convention.
30. A. Subbain, op.cit. pp. 160-161.
31. *Ibid.*, pp. 149-150.
32. *Ibid.*, p. 161.
33. *Ibid.*, p. 153.
34. Leah Levin, op.cit., p.538
35. A. Subbian, op.cit., p.170.
36. Leah Levin, op.cit., p. 539.
37. A. Subbian, op.cit., pp. 181-183.
38. *Ibid.*, pp. 211-229.
39. *National Institutions for the Promotion and Protection of Human Rights*, Fact Sheet No. 19, UN Centre for Human Rights, (New York and Geneva: 1995).

40. *Ibid.*

41. Report of the Secretary-General : Strengthening of the UN – An Agenda for Further Change, 9 September, 2002, Doc. A/57/387, para 50.

42. Orest J.W. Nowosad, "The ABC of National Human Rights Institutions" in *Journal of the NHRC,* Vol. 5 (2006), p. 72.

Chapter II

Institutionalisation of Human Rights : Making of the NHRC

Internationalisation of human rights began with the Universal Declaration of Human Rights in December 1948. Since then, the United Nations has played a pivotal role in standards and norms-setting in the field of human rights. The decades of 1960s and 1970s were largely concerned with evolving human rights jurisprudence and developing international monitoring system for the implementation of human rights. But the experience of international monitoring bodies was not to the satisfaction of the world body and civil society. Therefore, the emphasis was shifted from international approach to the regional and national approach in the decades of 1980s and 1990s. The concept of National Human Rights Institution (hereafter NHRI) is the outcome of these developments. Effective NHRIs with a broad mandate encompassing all human rights have the potential to complement at the national level, the vital monitoring and accountability role performed by the United Nations treaty bodies at the international level.[1]

Evolution of the NHRIs

It is true that NHRIs became a reality only in the 1990s, however, the seeds of this concept were sown half a century ago. At its second session, in 1946, the Economic and Social Council (hereafter ECOSOC) invited the member states 'to consider the desirability of establishing information groups or local human rights committees within their respective countries to collaborate with them in furthering the work of the commission on Human Rights.'[2] But it turned out to be a mere lip-service.

After a gap of fourteen years, again, the matter was put on the agenda of the ECOSOC which recognising the importance of the role of national institutions in the promotion and protection of human rights called upon the governments to encourage the formation and continuation of such bodies as well as to communicate all relevant information on the subject to the Secretary-General.[3] Nothing worthwhile happened in this regard except the exchange of reports between the Secretary-General, the Commission on Human Rights, General Assembly and the states.

The first serious attempt, to move on from the rhetorics to reality, with regard to the establishment of the national institutions, was made, in 1978, when a seminar was convened in Geneva, by the Commission on Human Rights to draft the guidelines for the structure and functioning of national institutions.[4] The draft guidelines, prepared by this seminar, were duly endorsed by the Commission on Human Rights and the General Assembly. The efforts were made, throughout 1980s, to take appropriate steps for the establishment of national institutions for the promotion and protection of human rights.

Consequently, a number of national institutions were established – most often with the assistance of the Advisory Services Programme of the Centre for Human Rights. Armenia, Azerbaijan and Georgia in the Caucasus received help to strengthen the human rights structures in their countries.

In 1991, the Commission on Human Rights held a workshop for the national and regional institutions engaged in the promotion and protection of human rights to review patterns of cooperation between national institutions and international organisations, and to explore ways of increasing the effectiveness of national institutions. The conclusions of the workshop, held in Paris, were endorsed by the Commission on Human Rights[5] as the principles relating to the status of national institutions (hereafter Paris Principles) and also accepted by the General Assembly.[6]

Paris Principles affirm that national institutions are to be vested with competence to promote and protect human rights and given as broad a mandate as possible, set forth clearly in a constitutional or legislative text. The principles represent a refinement and extension of the guidelines framed in 1978.[7]

The agenda of national institutions was vigorously followed since 1991. A number of important meetings were convened to promote the cause of national institutions.[8] During the course of preparation for the 1993 World Conference on Human Rights, a parallel meeting of national institutions was held to examine the purposes of national institutions, the key requisites for appropriate and effective functioning including representative nature and accessibility and mechanisms for coordinating inter-institutional activities.[9]

The World Conference on Human Rights, 1993 through the Vienna Declaration and Programme of Action reaffirmed the important and constructive role played by national institutions for the promotion and protection of human rights, in particular, in their advisory capacity to the competent authorities, their role in remedying human rights violations, in the dissemination of human rights information, and education in human rights.[10] Recognising the right of each state to choose the framework which is best suited to its particular needs at the national level, it encouraged the establishment and strengthening of national institutions.[11] It further recommended the strengthening of United Nations activities and programmes to meet requests for assistance from states in the establishment or strengthening of national institutions.[12]

Besides the United Nations system, several other international organisations have also been active in promoting the establishment and development of national human rights institutions. Prominent among these are the Commonwealth Secretariat and the International Ombudsman Institute. The Commonwealth has sponsored a number of international and national workshops and also developed extensive material including a directory of existing institutions in Commonwealth countries and a manual for guidance to the states wishing to establish new institutions.[13]

Thus, the national human rights institutions have emerged globally as effective regulatory and monitoring devices for the implementation and promotion of human rights at the national level, helping translate the rhetorics of human rights into reality.

Conceptual Meaning of National Human Rights Institutions

Despite the fact that the concept of national human rights institutions is almost half a century old, yet there is no agreed definition of the term 'national human rights institution.' The reason is that the concept has undergone an evolutionary change in terms of its framework. Initially, it meant 'to include virtually any institution at the national level having a direct or indirect impact on the promotion and protection of human rights,'[14] taking into its ambit judiciary, administrative tribunals, legislative organs, non-governmental organisations, legal aid offices, social welfare schemes, national advisory commissions, ombudsman offices and related structures. Gradually, this broad framework narrowed down on the basis of particular common functions such as educational-promotional, advisory, investigative and grievance redressal. Still, this functional approach to categorisation failed to impart a specific meaning or definition to what constitutes a national institution for the promotion and protection of human rights.

It was with the Paris Principles that a normative framework for national institutions emerged. As per this framework, 'a national institution must be a body established in the constitution or by law to perform particular functions in the field of human rights.'[15] The NHRIs are independent bodies whose composition and mandate are well-defined in the national constitution and/or legislation. They are 'the primary mechanisms for translating international human rights norms into a local culture of human rights.'[16] They are entrusted with the task of monitoring the works of government from within and impressing upon them to carry out their treaty obligations under the international human rights conventions.

The Paris Principles define the criteria for functions, composition, financing and other elements for ensuring the independent and effective functioning of the national institutions. These norms focus on three general areas : (i) the competence and responsibilities of national institutions, concerning their legislative foundation as well as their primary tasks; (ii) the composition of national institutions and the guarantees of independence and pluralism, listing criteria for appointment designed to ensure plurality of representation as well as financial independence; and (iii) the methods of operation of national institutions including the mandate to take up matters as well as their cooperation with civil society. Apart from these elements, a specific section was added; (iv) relating particularly to those institutions with quasi-jurisdictional competence, i.e., the competence to hear, transmit and settle individual complaints.[17]

Thus, the Paris Principles have imparted a definite meaning to the concept of national human rights institutions. Now, for the purposes of United Nations activities in the field of human rights[18] and for the purpose of definition, a national human rights institution comprises those institutions which comply with the principles relating to the status of national institutions, or the Paris Principles.[19]

Nomenclature of NHRIs

Like in the case of definition, the NHRIs lack unanimity in the matter of nomenclature as well. They are known by different names in different countries. There are three main classes in which majority of NHRIs are placed : human rights commission, ombudsman and specialised institutions.

Human Rights Commissions deal with one or more specific functions directly related to the promotion and protection of human rights, including an advisory function (regarding law and government policy on human rights), an educative function and impartial investigative function. It is not common for a human rights commission to possess an authority to impose a legally binding verdict on parties to a complaint.[20]

The institution of ombudsman is primarily associated with impartial investigative function to oversee fairness and legality in public administration. Of late, some of them have been given specific human rights protection mandates in relation to the rights set in the national constitutions or other legislation.[21]

The specialised human rights institutions are established to promote and protect the rights of vulnerable groups in the society such as children, women, disabled, refugees, minorities and indigeneous population, etc. These institutions undertake activities to promote government and social policy concerning the rights of vulnerable groups together with advisory, educative, proactive and investigative role. They are also responsible for monitoring the effectiveness of existing laws and constitutional provisions relating to vulnerable groups. They are rarely empowered to make binding decisions or to initiate legal action.[22]

The national human rights institutions do not include those organisations which are established with political purposes and lack independence and fairness. The NHRIs need to abide by the Paris Principles for structural and jurisdictional framework purposes. The NHRIs may be local/national institutions but they have acquired an international status and therefore, they are expected to meet the international standards spelt out as the Paris Principles.

NHRIs - The Global Scenario

There were a few national human rights institutions in existence before the adoption of the Paris Principles. The oldest one was established in France in 1948.[23] Later on, in the 1970s and 1980s, some other countries also established similar institutions, such as, New Zealand (1978), Canada (1978), Australia (1981 re-established in 1986), the Philippines (1987) and Denmark (1987).

The national human rights institutions have become the focal point for implementation of human rights standards after the adoption of the Paris Principles in 1991 and the Vienna Declaration in 1993, leading to the establishment of such institutions globally.

The decade of 1990s witnessed an upsurge in the establishment of national human rights institutions in almost all the regions round the globe. In the African continent, broadly mandated national institutions have been established in Cameroon (1991), Chad (1994), Ghana (1993), Nigeria (1996), Senegal (1997), South Africa (1995), Uganda (1996) and Zambia (1997).[24] In the Asia-Pacific region, India (1993), Indonesia (1994) and Sri Lanka (1997) have set up these institutions. In the Latin American region, Mexico (1990) and Costa Rica (1993) possessed such institutions. In Europe, Latvia (1995) is the only country with national institution. Similarly, in the CIS (Commonwealth of Independent States of the former Soviet Union) region, broadly mandated institutions have been established in Kazakhstan (1996) and Georgia (1997).

In addition, many more countries are planning to have such institutions in near future. They include Bangladesh, Ethopia, Federal Republic of Germany, Fiji, Ireland, Kyrgyzstan, Liberia, Malawi, Mongolia, Nepal, Pakistan, Papua New Guinea, Rwanda, Tanzania, Thailand and Uzbekistan. Thus, the process of institutionalisation of human rights which began at the international level has seeped down to the national / local level in the form of national human rights institutions.

Establishment of the NHRC in India

India's commitment to human rights dates back to the national freedom struggle days and it extends beyond the national frontier as well. India was the first country led by Mahatma Gandhi to raise a voice against the practice of racial discrimination in South Africa. After the Independence, India adopted a republican constitution guaranteeing fundamental rights to its citizens. Also, it has been an active participant in the international deliberations on human rights issues at various fora and signatory to many of the international covenants and conventions on human rights. Adding to it, the presence of a free press and judiciary as also an active non-governmental human rights community lends a legitimacy to its democratic base.

Despite the above favourable background, the ground reality at the implementation level is very aptly described by Justice Krishna Iyer as 'human rights in peaceful coexistence with inhuman violations.'[25] In the post-Independence period, there was hardly any public awareness about human rights. So, the practice of human rights abuses committed in the name of curbing Naxalite menace or fighting insurgencies in the North-East went unnoticed in the public eyes. But the massive abuse of human rights of masses experienced during the infamous 'Emergency Rule' of 1975-1977, helped in spelling out the true significance of human rights to the people in general. Thus, the experience of 'Emergency Rule' became instrumental in the emergence of human rights movement in the country, resulting in the appearance of various human rights groups and organisations.

Tracing the history of human rights groups / organisations, the first such organisation existed in the pre-independence era. Formed by Pt Jawaharlal Nehru in the early 1930s, it was named Civil Liberties Union and worked to collect information on human rights violations and to provide legal aid to the nationalists faced with the charge of sedition by the then British government. Madras Civil Liberties Organisation was formed in 1947 to perform similar activities.

In the post-Independence days, Civil Liberties Committee, in Calcutta was formed to fight the repression of Communists nationwide consequent to the ban imposed on their activities. In the 1960s, some human rights organisations became active in the area of the rights of traditionally oppressed people. The Association for Protection of Democratic Rights (APDR) in 1972 at Calcutta and the Andhra Pradesh Civil Liberties Committee (APCLC) in 1974 became active in fighting the excesses committed by the state.

The real human rights activism was seen during and after the Emergency period when a spate of human rights organisations / groups surfaced to protect and promote human rights. These included Citizens for Democracy (CFD), People's Union for Civil Liberties (PUCL), People's Union for Democratic Rights (PUDR), the Free Legal Aid Committee (FLAC), the Civil Liberties and Human Rights Organisation, Manipur, The Jammu and Kashmir People's Movement for Human Rights and many more. They carried out varied functions such as fact-finding or investigation, public interest litigation, free legal aid, public awareness programme, campaigns for human right causes, preparation of supportive literature for independent movements and organisations.[26] These organisations played a vital role in bringing the issue of human rights to the fore in public debates. The human rights jurisprudence and judicial activism witnessed during this period provided further impetus to human rights movement.

Together with these efforts, a political initiative was taken in 1977 by the Janata Party including a proposal to set up a Civil Rights Commission, in its Election Manifesto. The proposed commission, to be headed by a person equivalent to the rank of a Supreme Court Judge, would have been an independent and autonomous body. It was also proposed to merge the Scheduled Castes and Tribes Commission and the Minorities Commission into the new institution and entrust the proposed commission to discharge the role assigned to these bodies.[27]

In 1980s, various other proposals were made from time to time to institutionalise a human rights system of investigation, monitoring and enforcement of human rights at the national level in the form of a commission or tribunal. The Minorities Commission, in 1983, made a recommendation for a comprehensive National Integration-cum-Human Rights Commission, having a constitutional madate.[28] In 1985, the then Chief Justice of India, P.N. Bhagwati, also made a suggestion for the establishment of a National Human Rights Commission.[29] Again, in 1986, human right activists in the country proposed to constitute a Human Rights Tribunal comprising mainly of former judges to investigate violations of human rights.[30] Also, the renowned legal luminary, Dr L.M. Singhvi advocated for the creation of a Human Rights Commission in each state and at the national level in 1988.[31]

The above repeated demand for a national human rights institution was manifestation of the increasing public awareness and the widespread reporting of human rights abuses and their growing criticism at the national and international levels.[32] The most worrying aspect of it all was the defensive attitude of the government in face of the above criticism,[33] which added credence to the repeated demand for a national human rights commission at the earliest.

In 1991, the Congress Party made a promise in its election manifesto to establish a national human rights commission within one year of its assuming power.[34] The electoral commitment of the Congress Party soon turned into a compulsion for the congress government due to the ever-increasing external pressures on the issue of human rights. It was pointed out that 'by delaying the establishment of a human rights commission, the Indian government was only allowing further pressure from the western aid givers to be built up before the Aid-India Consortium meeting.'[35] In June 1992, the U.S. House of Representatives passed an amendment which reduced development aid for all countries guilty of human rights violations but which was regarded essentially as being anti-India in its origin.[36] The Republican senator who sponsored the amendment, made it known that he was doing so to voice his criticism of the human rights situation in India.[37] Earlier, in 1990, Republican Congressman, Dan Burton, had even sought to terminate all non-humanitarian aid to India being given by the USA for the same reason.[38] Similarly, Germany's stand on aid and human rights record had also become tougher around the same time.[39]

It cannot be denied that the process of establishing a human rights commission was expedited largely due to the external criticism and pressures from foreign donors. According to one analyst :

'The Commission is not being set up in response to any demand from Indian activists campaigning for civil or democratic rights. It is to meet the criticism of India's human rights record by the Western aid donors. It would save Mr. Stephen Solarz, former New York Congressman, of having to oppose cuts in United States to aid. Last time, an amendment for a marginal docking of aid to India came up, Mr Solarz entered his apologia for New Delhi : Prime Minister, P.V. Narsimha Rao, had announced the decision to set up an independent, autonomous human rights organisation.'[40]

Not only this, by its own admission, the rationale of human rights commission lies in the need to dispell any impression of the government's lack of seriousness on the issue of human rights.[41]

Against this backdrop, the government embarked upon the process of establishing a human rights commission. In February 1992, the government made its intention clear that it proposed to set up a human rights commission by an Act of Parliament and the proposed legislation would be formulated after studying the structures of similar organisations in other countries.[42] The then Home Minister, Mr S.B. Chavan, stated in the Lok-Sabha that India would have 'its own' human rights commission. The only question the government had to decide was whether such a body should be officially appointed as its credibility had to be established.[43] Similar statement was made in the Rajya Sabha by the Home Minister who also proposed to discuss the proposed legislation with all the Chief-Ministers and also with leaders of different parties before hand.[44]

In September 1992, a conference of chief ministers was convened to discuss and deliberate on the proposed draft bill. The conference endorsed the proposal for a human rights commission and entrusted the task of drafting the proposed bill to a high-power committee comprising of five chief-ministers and some cabinet ministers which was asked to submit its report by the end of October 1992.[45]

Though the idea of a human rights commission was endorsed by the chief ministers' Conference but the various views expressed by the participants at the conference make the hesitant and cautious approach towards the proposed commission amply clear. Most chief ministers felt that it should not duplicate the work of the judiciary and should make use of the central and state investigative machineries. Mizoram Chief Minister, Lalthan Hwala, was opposed to the setting up of the commission as he felt that there were enough safeguards provided under the constitution to ensure the protection of human rights. The chief ministers, except from Uttar Pradesh, Bihar, Kerala and Andhra Pradesh, demanded that the jurisdiction of the commission should not overlap with the National Commission for Scheduled Castes and Tribes, Commission on Minorities and the Commission for Women, whereas the chief ministers of the BJP ruled states, i.e., Himachal Pradesh, Madhya Pradesh and Rajasthan wanted a single human rights commission to coordinate the functions of the existing commissions on the Scheduled Castes and Tribes, Minorities and Women. Andhra Pradesh Chief Minister, Janardhan Reddy, warned that the scope of the proposed commission should not come into conflict with the established institutions which discharged their functions under various statutes. On the one hand, Madhya Pradesh Chief Minister, Sunderlal Patwa opposed a central legislation for preventing custodial crimes on the ground that a state-level human rights commission was already operating and another legislation was not necessary; while on the other hand, Karnataka Chief Minister, S. Bangarappa, suggested the setting up of state level human rights commission and called for a clear demarcation of the jurisdiction between the national commission and the state-level commissions. Orissa Chief Minister, Biju Patnaik, was optimistic when he said that there was no doubt that the proposed commission would function as an authority as he believed that the state government would be accountable to it, especially as the commission would be set up by an Act of Parliament. Lastly, all chief ministers unequivocally expressed concern over the issue of human rights being used by separatists and militant groups to launch their propaganda against the security forces. Assam Chief Minister, Hiteshwar Saikia, was critical of some organisations and media men for reporting custodial crimes out of proportion while keeping mum over the human rights violations of citizens by the militants. Punjab Chief Minister, Beant Singh, cautioned against the commission getting reduced to a forum with only an advisory body. A note of caution was sounded by the Jammu and Kashmir Governor, Girish Saxena, who said that government was dealing with a proxy war under normal civil laws.[46]

Besides the Chief Ministers' Conference, a series of seminars were held in various parts of the country to elicit public opinion on the proposed human rights commission. Several questions regarding it came up for discussions. Should the scope of the human rights commission be limited to a specific set of rights or should it be wider? Should the human rights commission concern itself only with human rights violations by law-enforcing agencies or should the violations committed by influential sections of society and terrorist groups also be included in its ambit? Should the human rights commission have investigative powers or should its role be confined to fact-finding? Should the human rights commission have an independent investigative agency or should it employ the existing state apparatus (like the state police, CID and CBI)? Should the human rights commission have powers of adjudication? What should be the role of the human rights commission in respect of alleged human rights violations by armed/paramilitary forces, especially in insurgency affected areas? And, what should be the relationship of the human rights commission with non-governmental organisations (NGOs) engaged in the field of human rights?

With regard to these questions, the opinions of some prominent human rights activists, jurists and legal experts presented the non-official perception of the proposed human rights commission. Before the Act was enacted and ordinance was promulgated, the People's Union of Civil Liberties (PUCL) had discussed the various aspects of the proposed human rights commission in detail and the opinion was divided on whether such a commission would be of any use and if the provisions that were being circulated were sufficient. The final decision taken at the Mumbai National Convention of the PUCL welcomed the establishment of human rights commission as an institution created by an Act of Parliament. It considered it to be an achievement in itself despite some drawbacks which it believed could always be reformed and improved upon. Something is better than nothing. It, however, pointed out that such a commission was no substitute of organisations like the PUCL.[47]

At another seminar on the proposed human rights commission organised in New Delhi by the government, most of the non-official invitees were of the opinion that unless certain basic conditions were fulfilled, even prior to the constitution of the commission, doubts about motives of the government in forming the commission would not be dispelled. According to Justice Rajinder Sachar, 'An important question, however, is whether the commission should have investigative powers and its own investigative machinery or it should only make use of the machinery of the various state governments. Some well-meaning participants, though agreeing with the principle that unless the commission has its own investigating machinery, it would remain a lame duck, expressed anxiety that conferring power of investigation on the commission might amount to tresspassing on the states' exclusive power of legislation.[48]

Criticising the real motives behind the setting up a human rights commission, S.P. Sathe, termed it 'a cosmetic outfit' meant for obtaining a favourable testimonial on human rights by western donors. Calling it a defensive posture aimed at neutralising the criticism levelled by human rights organisations such as the Amnesty International (AI), Asia Watch and other national human rights non-governmental organisations, Sathe declared that the proposed human rights commission could not be a judicial body like the European Commission on Human Rights as its powers could not override those of the Supreme Court of India as well as the writ jurisdiction of the High Courts under Articles 32 and 226 of the Indian Constitution respectively. After weighing the constitutional limitations, he was of the view that the proposed commission would be a statutory body with powers similar to those given to the National Commission on Women under the National Commission of Women Act, 1990. In that case, its functions would be more of an investigative and recommendatory nature. In his opinion, the proposed commission to be an independent body, needed to be equipped with broad based membership, powers of appointment of chairperson and members be vested in an independent body headed by the Chief Justice of India, not with the government and having its own investigative machinery. Sathe wanted that the proposed commission should come through a constitutional amendment like the Finance Commission, not by statute like Women's Commission or by the government resolution like the Law Commission.[49]

According to another human rights activist, 'The setting up of a human rights commission as a response to criticism of the government's human rights record will at best be a formal act. It will not reduce human rights violations, but will be used to cover up such violations.'[50] He was of the view that human rights record could never improve by setting up of a commission without changing the existing social order. The debate on the setting up of a human rights commission should lead to a review of the functioning of the justice system and attempts had to be made to rebuild these institutions.[51]

Deploring the manner in which the government proceeded to set up the proposed human rights commission, several eminent jurists came out with a statement critical of 'the ill-conceived nature' of human rights commission which, they believed, would weaken rather than strengthen the existing democratic institutions and processes to defend human rights. The statement further included many useful suggestions for creating an effective and independent human rights commission.[52]

Another expert drew the attention to the difference between the promised human rights commission as per the Congress Party's election manifesto and the type of human rights commission proposed by the Union Home Minister, S.B. Chavan. As per the Congress' Manifesto pledge, 'The Congress will establish, by legislation, a Human Rights Commission to investigate and adjudicate complaints of violations of human rights, particularly the civil rights of groups or classes of people.' Pointing out the basic difference, he insisted that 'legislation' was necessary if a body was to be given power not only to 'investigate' but also to 'adjudicate', which was quite distinct from a Commission of Inquiry's power to inquire, report and recommend measures such a body should not be set up by an ordinance but only by a carefully considered bill.[53] The glaring contrast between the promised and the proposed human rights commission is indicative of the *raison d'etre* of the human rights commission in the eyes of government, i.e., 'to make use of its findings as correctives to the biased and one sided reports of the NGOs (non-governmental organisations) as well as to act as an effective answer to the politically motivated international criticism.'[54]

Divergent views that emerged as a result of ensuing public debate on the proposed human rights commission raised serious doubts about the real intention of the government in setting up of human rights commission which many in the human rights world looked upon as diabolical process to further restrict the sites of struggle available to the beleaguered citizenry.[55] In the proposed draft running into forty-five pages prepared by the Home Ministry, it outlined the restrictive functioning of the proposed body, i.e., it was barred to entertain cases which were subjudice and the armed forces and paramilitary forces were kept out of its jurisdiction, not empowered to entertain complaints certified by the competent authority as 'a matter of national security or public order not fit for public disclosure.'[56]

The feeling of distrust was mutual. The government was also skeptical of human rights groups. A recommendation made by the Amnesty International (AI) to Indian Government on the proposed human rights commission did not augur well with the government proposal as it recommended to exclude criminal actions by criminal organisations or by political groups resorting to arms as a means to achieve their goals and criminal actions occurring in the context of domestic violence, from the human rights commission's mandate and suggested separate mechanisms to these special crimes. The government considered it as a 'startling recommendation' because it implied that the human rights commission should not look into terrorist acts of various groups fighting for Khalistan, or secession of Assam or Kashmir from India. In other words, it was giving India a charter for dismemberment.[57]

Amidst this enraging controversy between the official and non-official perceptions of the proposed human rights commission, the Human Rights Commission Bill, 1993 was introduced in Lok-Sabha on 14th May, 1993. The Bill was referred to the Standing Committee of Parliament for the Ministry of Home Affairs. The Standing Committee invited suggestions by public notice and took evidence from experts. In response to its invitation, the committee received a number of memoranda from various persons. The Standing Committee also held a number of meetings in which officials of Law Ministry and Home Ministry were also invited. After clause by clause consideration of the bill and deliberations on the various suggestions received, the Standing Committee identified the issues which in its opinion required reconsideration.

Before the report of the Standing Committee could be presented in the Lok Sabha for the consideration of the House, an ordinance to provide for the constitution of a National Human Rights Commission and State Human Rights Commissions was promulgated on 28th September, 1993, reformulating the Original Bill in the light of extensive criticism aired during the proceedings of the Standing Committee. Pursuant to the promulgation of the Protection of Human Rights Ordinance, 1993, a five member National Human Rights Commission was constituted on 3rd October, 1993 which commenced its functioning from November 1993.

Meanwhile, a bill to replace the ordinance by an Act of Parliament was introduced in the Lok-Sabha on 9th December, 1993. Prior to that the Minister of State in the Ministry of Home Affairs, Shri P.M. Sayeed moved a resolution seeking the permission of the House to withdraw the original bill on 7th December, 1993. This move of the government elicited strong opposition and severe criticism of the manner in which government proceeded to set up a human rights commission in a hurried fashion both inside the parliament and outside it.

Inside the parliament, the government came in for criticism on technical grounds and the failure of Indian diplomacy in succumbing to external pressures. Besides raising the points of order on the rules of parliamentary procedure about the manner in which the original bill was sought to be withdrawn mid-way through the committee-stage, the opposition members wanted to know as to why the particular ordinance had been issued during the pendency of the bill. George Fernandes accused the government of bringing disgrace to the House by making a statement such as the one given in the explanatory memorandum which said :

'Since the government was committed to the early constitution of the National Human Rights Commission, and there had been widespread discussion and comment on this matter in various fora and the media including the United Nations, any further delay in its constitution would have attracted severe adverse comments from all quarters.'[58]

Another member, Jaswant Singh, also made it amply clear that though he would welcome the establishment of a human rights commission but not if it were on account of any external pressures, or on account of external considerations as had been evidenced repeatedly by the government's own statements verbally and in writing. He further charged the government of acquiescing to the pressure that came from the United States and others. As a consequence, the establishment of a human rights commission was a kind of fake and fraudulent public relation exercise without subscription to basic human rights.[59]

During the discussion on the resolution seeking to replace the Protection of Human Rights Ordinance, 1993 by the modified bill, several members in the Lok-Sabha questioned the rationale of the ordinance. They were not ready to accept the raison d'etre offered by the government in this regard. Smt Geeta Mukherjee was of the view that the promulgation of an ordinance would not help in anyway to stop Pakistan from using human rights card against India at various international fora. Instead, it had resulted in denying the House an opportunity to debate such an important matter.[60] Terming the renewed bill as a 'half-hearted effort', George Fernandes questioned the need of this bill. He also pointed out several shortcomings in the bill and urged the government to find suitable remedies.[61] Another member, Saifuddin Choudhury, also expressed his dissatisfaction at the fact that the commission was created through an ordinance while the bill was being discussed by the Standing Committee. He questioned, 'What was the hurry in doing so? Was it to satisfy some foreign powers? Or, is the Human Rights Commission to be there in the country for our own requirements?' In his view, a human rights commission is not a cosmetic thing; it is not an adhoc thing but it is the reflection of the fact that we, as a civilised society, want to guarantee the rights of the people; as a civilised state, want to ensure that the arms of the state do not injure the people, the community in a wrong way, in an uncivilized manner. He considered human rights commission as our own need.[62]

Outside the parliament, too, the government's move to set up a human rights commission by promulgation of an ordinance came in for sharp criticism. Accusing the government of expedient evasion of a debate, one analyst opined, 'Two immediate conclusions are possible about the national commission on the human rights. First, an ordinance has hurriedly put it into place in anticipation of an intensified campaign by the US-Pakistan combine on the human rights issue in Kashmir. Second, by failing to satisfy the human rights activists, both foreign and home grown, it has provided them with more things to grumble about. Already, it is being said that commission is heavily weighed in favour of the government point of view.'[63] Justice Krishna Iyer also characterised the setting up of the National Human Rights Commission as National Human Rights Omission.[64]

Despite all this criticism, the bill replacing the Protection of Human Rights Ordinance,1993 was finally passed by both the Houses of Parliament and received the President's assent on 8th January, 1994. And, at last, it found its place on the statute book as the Protection of Human Rights Act, 1993 (10 of 1994).

In view of the above stated facts, it becomes obvious that the establishment of the National Human Rights Commission has not been without controversies and criticisms particularly against the government as its intentions were doubted whether it concerned the motives, the manner and the terms of reference with regard to the National Human

Rights Commission. Initially, the state was accused of indulging in human rights abuses and not doing enough to protect and promote human rights in the country. And when it agreed to have a national human rights commission to look into the complaints of human rights violations, doubts were raised about its sincerity and the motives. The hurried manner in which the government tried to install a national human rights commission further exposed it to the charge of being out of appease foreign donors. Similarly, in the matter of terms of reference of the national human rights commission, the government was accused of indulging in cosmetic exercise.

However, the establishment of the National Human Rights Commission has been a great milestone in the journey of human rights movement in the country. Whatever critics may say about the motive, manner and mandate of the National Human Rights Commission, the fact remains that it could not have come a day sooner. The compulsion of the circumstances made it happen, whether it be internal requirement or foreign donors' pressure. But whatever happened, happened for the good. The end product turned out to be a model institution in the world of national human rights institutions. It can be seen as an endorsement of the Paris Principles[65] and the Vienna Declaration.[66]

References

1. Earle Patrick, "Human Rights Council of Europe", *National Human Rights Institutions and The Human Rights Approach to Development*, 2.
2. Economic and Social Council resolution 2/9 of 21 June 1946, Sect. 5.
3. Economic and Social Council resolution 772B (XXX) of 25 July, 1960.
4. See ST/HR/SER. A/2 and Add.1.
5. Vide resolution 1992/54.
6. Vide G.A. resolution 48/134 of 20 December, 1993.
7. *Establishment and Strengthening of National Institutions for the Promotion and Protection of Human Rights*, Professional Series No.4, Centre for Human Rights, (Geneva : 1995), p. 5.
8. The Second United Nations Workshop for the Asian-Pacific Region on Human Rights Issues (Jakarta, January 1993); the Meeting of Representatives of National Institutions and Organisations Promoting Tolerance and Harmony and Combating Racism and Racial Discrimination (Sydney, April 1993); and the Second International Workshop on National Institutions for Promotion and Protection of Human Rights (Tunis, December 1993).

9. Supra no. 7, para 29, p. 5.
10. The Vienna Declaration and Programme of Action, 1993, Part I, para 36.
11. *Ibid.*
12. Supra no.7, para 31, pp. 5-6.
13. *Ibid.*, paras 33-35, p. 6
14. *Ibid.*, para 36.
15. *Ibid.*, para 38.
16. A.S. Anand, "Role of National Human Rights Institutions : Indian Experience", *Journal of the National Human Rights Commission*, Vol. 4 (New Delhi : 2005), p. 57.
17. Birgit Lindsnaes and Lone Lindholt, "National Human Rights Institutions, Standard Setting and Achievements" in *National Human Rights Institutions* (eds.) Lindsnaes et.al. Danish Center for Human Rights, 2000, pp. 10-11.
18. The term 'national institution' as defined under Paris Principles is accepted. See Supra n.7, para 39, p. 6.
19. Orest J.W. Nowosad, "The ABC of National Human Rights Institutions", *Journal of the National Human Rights Commission*, Vol. 5 (2006), (New Delhi), p. 50.
20. Supra. no.7, paras 46-52, pp. 7-8.
21. *Ibid.*, paras 56-61, p. 8.
22. *Ibid.*, paras 53-55, p. 8.
23. The French Commission was established as a consultative body to the Government at the initiative of Rene Cassin, judicial advisor of General de Gaulle. In 1984, the Commission was reactivated and in 1993 the Commission achieved 'independent' status by constitutional decree.
24. According to the Report of the Chairman of the Coordinating Committee of African National Institutions for the Second Conference of African National Institutions; Durban, South Africa (1-3 July, 1998), there are about 20 African national institutions.
25. V.R. Krishna Iyer, "Dream or Reality?" in *Seminar* (405) May 1993, p. 36.
26. Smitu Kothari, "The Human Rights Movement in India : A Critical Overview", *Social Action* Vol. 40 (January-March 1990), pp. 2-4.
27. Arun K. Palai, *"National Human Rights Commission in India"*, (New Delhi : 1998), pp. 45-46.

28. "Panel urged on Human Rights Integration", *The Times of India* (New Delhi), 20 April, 1983.

29. Manoranjan Mohanty, "The Fight for Rights : Race of Civil Liberties Groups", *The Statesman* (New Delhi), 15 September, 1985.

30. "Plan to Form Human Rights Tribunal", *The Indian Express* (New Delhi), 30 June, 1986.

31. *The Statesman* (New Delhi), 20 March, 1988.

32. Nagaland File : Question of Human Rights, by Nandita Haksar and Luigam Luithule (New Delhi : 1984); Reports of the Tarkunde and Bhargava Commissions exposing encounter killings of Naxalites in Andhra Pradesh; India : Torture, Rape and Deaths in Custody, Amnesty International's Report (New Delhi) March 1992; and The Crackdown in Kashmir : Torture of Detainees and Assaults on the Medical Community, A Joint Publication by 'Physicians for Human Rights' and Asia Watch, USA.

33. In 1988, the then Prime-Minister, Late Rajiv Gandhi categorically denied the reported complaints of custodial torture as true. (An Interview on the British television programme 'Panorama' in January 1988. Similarly, Prime-Minister, Late P.V. Narsimha Rao, in early 1992 remarked that human rights organisations were concerned only with the human rights of terrorists, not about the human rights of victims of terrorist violence. (Address to the National Integration Council, quoted in *Seminar* (405), May 1993, p. 21. Also, V.N. Gadgil, "Upholding Human Rights : Distorted deliberations at Geneva Talking shop" in *Indian Express* (New Delhi), April 1, 1992.

34. *Manifesto of the Indian National Congress*, Lok Sabha Elections, 1991 [AICC (I)], 24 Akbar Road, New Delhi, p. 62.

35. "Pressure on India on human rights", *The Times of India,* (New Delhi), 8 June, 1992.

36. Vijay S.T. Shankardass, "Living upto our commitment" in *Seminar* (405), May 1993, p. 21.

37. *Ibid.*

38. *Ibid.*

39. Supra, no. 35.

40. "Placating the West" by Mohan Ram, *The Pioneer* (New Delhi), 4 October, 1993.

41. A background note of the Home Ministry as quoted by Mohan Ram, op.cit.

42. "Human Rights – Plan to setup commission", *Times of India* (New Delhi), 5 February, 1992.
43. "India to have human rights commission", *The Statesman* (New Delhi), 6 March, 1992.
44. Rajya Sabha Debates, Vol. 162, Nos. 16-20, dated 16 March, 1992, p.19.
45. "Human Rights body to be set up by October", *The Telegraph* (Calcutta), September 15, 1992.
46. *Ibid;* Also the report of the Chief Ministers' Conference on Human Rights, Ministry of Home Affairs, Government of India (New Delhi), September 1992.
47. Y.P. Chhibbar, "National Human Rights Commission : A View from People's Front", in *Human Rights : Fifty Years of India's Independence*, (ed.) K.P.Saxena, (New Delhi : 1999), pp. 119-120.
48. "Human Rights : Investigative Powers of the Panel." *Hindustan Times* (New Delhi), 27 November, 1992.
49. "Towards an Effective Human Rights Commission", *Economic and Political Weekly* (New Delhi), 3 October, 1992, pp. 2155-2156.
50. K.G. Kannabiran, "Why a Human Rights Commission?" *Economic and Political Weekly* (New Delhi), 26 September, 1992, pp. 2092-94.
51. *Ibid.*
52. "On Human Rights Commission" A Statement issued in Delhi after a consultation on human rights commission. The signatories included former judges V.R. Krishna Iyer, Rajinder Sachar, V.M. Tarkunde and Mr. D. Gana Pragasam. *Patriot* (Delhi), 31 March, 1992.
53. "Human Rights in India : How to make the proposed HRC more effective" by A.G. Noorani in *Indian Express* (New Delhi), 20 July, 1992.
54. V.N. Gadgil, the Congress Party spokesman as quoted in A.G. Noorani, supra no. 53.
55. *Seminar* (405), May 1993, p.13.
56. "Draft on human rights body finalised." *Telegraph* (Calcutta), 10 February, 1993.
57. "Commission or Omission" *Statesman* (New Delhi), 15 November, 1992.
58. Lok Sabha Debates, Vol. XXVI, Nos. 1-5, 7 December, 1992, p. 516.
59. *Ibid.*, p.522.
60. Lok-Sabha Debates, Vol. XXVII, Nos. 10-12, 14 December, 1992, p. 393.

61. *Ibid.*, pp. 405-418.
62. *Ibid.*, p. 427.
63. N.J. Nanporia, "National Commission on Human Rights : Expedient Evasion of a Debate", *Newstimes* (Bombay), 23 October, 1993.
64. Quoted by Harsh Sethi in *Seminar* (405), May 1993, p.12.
65. Supra no. 5.
66. Supra no. 11.

Chapter III

Organisation, Powers and Functions of the NHRC

Sigmund Freud once famously observed, 'Anatomy is destiny.'[1] Although made in a different context, this remark is true for statutory bodies also. For a National Institution, its anatomy is, in a sense, contained in the Act that establishes it. The NHRC has been established under the Protection of Human Rights Act, 1993 and its anatomy is contained in this Act.

The Objects and Reasons as stated in the Act, have set a high goal for the NHRC. Here an attempt is being made to examine whether the anatomy of NHRC helps, rather than inhibits or lends itself to inhibit the proper fulfillment of its destiny, i.e., the fulfillment of the goals set therein.

The nature of the task assigned to the NHRC is such that it requires a nationwide institutional framework to facilitate easy accessibility to all for the redressal of complaints concerning human rights violation anywhere in the country. Under the Act, the mechanisms provided for the quick and effective implementation of human rights are in consonance with the federal nature of the Indian State.

The three-tier organisation system is adopted for this purpose. At the top-most level is the National Human Rights Commission; the State Human Rights Commissions fall at the middle level; and the District Committees and Human Rights Courts are provided for at the local level. Thus, a nationwide institutional structure is provided for by the Act[2] (Diagram No. 3.1).

Diagram No. 3.1

Nationwide Human Rights Institutional Framework

The Protection of Human Rights Act, 1993

Provides for the Constitution

of

The National Human Rights Commission Section 3	State Human Rights Commission Section 21	District Human Rights Committee & Human Rights Courts Section 30

For better protection of human rights and for the matters connected with their functioning

Source : The Protection of Human Rights Act and Relating Laws.

By : Mangari Rajendar (Hyderabad : 2000).

Definition of the Term "Human Rights"

As per the Act, 'human rights' means the rights relating to life, liberty, equality and dignity of the individual guaranteed by the Constitution or embodied in the international covenants and enforceable by courts of India.[3] Further, the Act also defines that 'international covenants' means the international covenant on civil and political rights and the international covenant on economic, social and cultural rights adopted by the General Assembly of the United Nations on 16th December, 1966.[4]

The above given definitions of the term 'human rights' and 'international covenants' are very narrow meaning and restrictive in scope. Because the term 'human rights', as defined by the Act, implies that only civil and political rights as enshrined in the Constitution under the category of fundamental rights qualify to be treated as human rights. Meaning thereby, that the NHRC cannot entertain any matter under the Directive Principles of State Policy[5] as they are non-justiciable rights. Similarly, the term 'international covenants' as defined by the Act, circumscribes the scope of human rights within the parameters of the two covenants only and fails to include other human rights related international conventions within its ambit. This is indicative of the narrow approach adopted by the Act and it limits the scope of the NHRC. Not only that, but it goes against the universality of human rights as pronounced by the Universal Declaration of Human Rights.

This weakness of the Act was recognised by the NHRC right at the very start of its functioning. It has sought amendments in the Act to give a broader meaning to these terms and expand the scope of human rights under the Act. According to the amendment recommended by the NHRC, the Section 2(1) (d) is reformulated as :

'Human Rights' means the rights relating to life, liberty, equality and dignity of the individual guaranteed by the constitution or embodied in the international covenants, conventions and treaties to which India is a party.[6]

The NHRC has also made a recommendation to delete Section 2(1)(f), so as to expand the definition of international covenants.[7] These specific amendments suggested by the NHRC in its very first annual report and were repeated in its second and third reports with a view to removing ambiguities and impediments concerning the competence of the NHRC. It may be pointed out here that the suggested amendments are in keeping with the law of land as laid down by the Supreme Court in a landmark judgement, in which it was held :

> 'Any international convention, not inconsistent with the fundamental rights and in harmony with their spirit must be read into these provisions to enlarge the meaning and content thereof...regard must be had to international conventions and norms for construing domestic law when there is no inconsistency between them and there is a void in domestic laws.'[8]

Yet, no action has been taken to give effect to these recommendations of the NHRC by the government for one or other reason. Still, this weakness of the statute has not come in the way of working of the NHRC which has adopted a liberal and progressive approach in dealing with human rights issues.

Composition of the Nhrc

The success of any institution/organisation depends on the competence and strength of the people who are manning the organisation. For the success of NHRC, it is necessary that it should be manned by the persons who can ensure its independence, impartiality and integrity.

Considering this, the Act provides for the following composition of the NHRC:

(i) A Chairperson who as been a Chief Justice of the Supreme Court;

(ii) One Member who is, or has been a judge of the Supreme Court;

(iii) One Member who is, or has been the Chief Justice of a High Court;

(iv) Two Members to be appointed from amongst persons having knowledge of, or practical experience in, matters relating to human rights.

(v) The Chairpersons of the National Commission for Minorities, the National Commission for the Scheduled Castes and Scheduled Tribes, and the National Commission for Women shall be deemed to be Members of the Commission for the discharge of functions specified in clauses (b) to (j) of section 12.

(vi) There shall be a Secretary-General who shall be the Chief Executive Officer of the Commission and shall exercise such power and discharge such functions of the Commission as it may delegate to him.[9]

Though, the Act has provided for a eight-membered commission, but the experience of the past-five years shows that there has always been vacancies waiting to be filled for the efficient working of the full commission. Not only that, but the provision, regarding the appointment of two members from amongst persons having knowledge of, or practical experience in matters relating to human rights, is also not adhered to. So far no such members have been appointed.

This attitude does not augur well with the provisions of the Paris Principles where it is clearly mentioned that the membership of the NHRIs should ensure wide representation of civil society groupings.[10] The constitution of the NHRC devoid of the representation of human rights activists has become a point of criticism. According to one commentator, 'It is desirable to make it mandatory appointment of two members who are having knowledge and practical experience of human rights.'[11]

The composition of the NHRC is also criticised as it does not reflect the country's sociological and political pluralism – a requirement emphasised by both the *UN Handbook* and the *Paris Principles.*[12] It has been regretted that it has so far not chosen either a human rights activist or a woman to the commission under the category of members having knowledge and practical experience in human rights. The only avenue for challenging the voices of vulnerable groups such as women, children, untouchables, etc. to the commission is through the ex-officio members of the commission.[13]

Procedure of Appointment of Chairperson and Other Members

The procedure of appointment of chairperson and other members of the NHRC is of great significance in determining the credibility of the institution. It gives a clear signal to the public about a national institution's independence. That is why, Paris Principles point out, 'An appointment process that includes the legislature and the public is likely to be independent, and to be perceived as such. Appointments made purely by the executive in a state have the potential to undermine efforts to establish an independent 'watch-dog.'[14] The appointment process should be as transparent as possible.

As per the Act, the chairperson and the other members of the NHRC are appointed by the President of India upon the recommendations of a committee.[15] This committee consists of :

(a)	The Prime Minister	-	Chairperson
(b)	Speaker of the House of the People	-	Member
(c)	Minister-in-charge of the Ministry of Home Affairs in the Government of India	-	Member
(d)	Leader of the Opposition in the House of the People	-	Member
(e)	Leader of the Opposition in the Council of States	-	Member
(f)	Deputy Chairperson of the Council of States[16]	-	Member.

The Act is silent on the procedure by which the committee would arrive at the decision and make recommendation about the appointment of the chairperson and the other members of the NHRC. The practice followed by the committee is that recommendations are decided by vote, not unanimously. This has become a cause of controversy.

Certain appointments should be unanimous. When they are not, they reflect a kind of politics which is parochial and petty. It was in 1999 when the chairmanship of the NHRC was decided by vote for the first time. The selection-committee comprised of the Speaker, the Prime Minister, the Home Minister, the Deputy Chairperson of Rajya Sabha and the Opposition leaders of both the House. The former Chief Justice, Mr J.C. Verma was selected by three-two votes. The Speaker, Mr Balyogi, the Prime Minister, Mr AtalBihari Vajpayee, and the Home Minister, Mr L.K. Advani, went in favour of Mr Verma. But the opposition leaders in the Lok Sabha and the

Rajya Sabha, Ms Sonia Gandhi, and Mr Manmohan Singh, opposed him. The Deputy Chairperson, Ms Najma Heptullah, was abroad. Had she been present, she would have probably followed her party-line. Then, it would have been a tie : three votes in favour and three against.[17]

The rules do not say whether the Speaker or the Prime Minister has the casting vote. The Attorney-General, Mr Soli Sorabji, too, was not sure whether there was a provision of casting vote. The President was said to have queried why the meeting was held when the Deputy Chairperson of the Rajya Sabha, way away. Whether it was chance or deliberate that the meeting was fixed when Ms Heptullah was away might not be known. But when a panel comprises of six members, it should be laid down what will happen if there is a tie.[18]

Perhaps, this kind of politicisation of the appointments was foreseen by the experts. That is why they were critical of the selection – committee as mooted by the Act. According to an expert, 'After narrowly circumscribing the categories from which the members of the NHRC will be chosen, it is no consolation that their actual selection is left to a six-member committee. Of them, four will be from the ruling party – the Prime Minister, the Home Minister, the Speaker of the Lok Sabha and the Deputy Chairman of the Rajya Sabha. The other two will be the leaders of the opposition from both Houses of Parliament."[19] He suggested, 'Since it is a quasi-judicial body concerned with a sensitive subject, why not leave the nominations to the President from a panel drawn up by the Chief Justice of India, the next senior most judge and the Chief Justice of a High Court nominated by his peers?'[20]

According to another view, "Chairperson of the commission is not the member of the selection committee and does not have 'any say' in appointment of the members of the commission. It is desirable to have the 'say' of the chairperson in the appointment of the Members of the Commission, as the chairperson has to work with them in discharging duties. Atleast there should be some provision that the chairperson of the commission should be consulted while selecting the members."[21]

The above criticism of the selection process of the chairman and other members of the NHRC as laid down by the Act, has raised certain valid points about the politicisation of selection process. But the blame lies with the persons, not with the composition of the selection committee and with the selection process. It is really unfortunate that they cannot spare even an institution like NHRC to remain above party-politics and not to make an issue of appointments to the NHRC. The selection process as laid down by the Act follows the guidelines of the Paris Principles[22] wherein it is stated clearly that an appointment process could involve the establishment of a special and fully representative parliamentary committee to handle the selection process. The Act has further provided for the consultation with the Chief Justice of India in the case of consideration for appointment of a sitting Judge of the Supreme Court or sitting Chief Justice of a High Court. Thus, the procedure of appointment as laid by the Act is designed to secure the best possible members. It has also been stated in the Act that no appointment of a chairperson or a member shall be invalid merely by reason of any vacancy in the committee. Therefore, the selection process facilitates the appointment of the chairperson and other members of the NHRC.

Removal of a Member of the NHRC

The Paris Principles demand that commissioners should not be removed except for reasons specified in the enabling law. These reasons, and the method of removal, should be parallel to those applicable to members of the judiciary.[23] Pursuant to these guidelines, the chairperson and the members of the NHRC cannot be removed from office except as in the manner prescribed by the Act. Under the Act, only the President of India has the power to remove the chairperson or any other member of the NHRC from office for reasons of misbehaviour or incapacity to perform their duties.[24] The procedure for the removal as laid down in the Act requires a referral by the President of India to the Supreme Court for conducting an inquiry into the allegations of misbehaviour or incapacity against the Chairperson or any member of the NHRC in accordance with the procedure prescribed by it and make recommendation to the President on the basis of any of the grounds found to be true. However, the above provision has no bar on the President to remove the chairperson or the members of the commission on any of the following grounds if they are :

(1) adjudged as an insolvent; or

(2) engaged in any paid employment outside during their term of office; or

(3) unfit to continue in office by reasons of infirmity of mind and body; or

(4) declared as of unsound mind by a competent court of law; or

(5) convicted or sentenced to imprisonment for an offence which in the opinion of the President involves moral turpitude.[25]

The tough procedure of removal as prescribed under the Act, surpasses the Paris Principles criteria and helps in ensuring the independence of the NHRC.

Terms of Appointment and Service of the Members and Chairperson

As per the guidelines issued under the Paris Principles, the terms of appointment and conditions of service of the chairperson and other members of the NHRIs deal with the duration of tenure, re-appointment issue and privileges and immunities. These guidelines provide for fixed term of appointment, continuity in the membership of NHRIs, protection of the members from employment related repraisal of work performed in the line of duty and duration of tenure long enough to permit the members to hone expertise and to make use of expertise for the benefit of the public.[26]

The Act provides for a five year term of office of the chairperson from the date he/she assumes the charge or until he/she attains the age of seventy years, whichever is earlier. Same terms are applicable on the appointment of members of the NHRC but members can be reappointed for another term. However, no member shall hold office after he /she attains the age of seventy years.

Although, this provision relating to the duration of tenure fulfils the criterion provided by the Paris Principles, yet some people find some problem with it. According to one human right activist, 'A situation can be visualised in which there may be no person qualified to be the chief of the commission. The chairperson has to be a person who has been the chief Justice of the Supreme Court and has to be less than seventy years of age. Mr Justice Ranganath Mishra retired when he had served only for two and half years because he achieved (sic.) the age of seventy years. When he retired, there was only one person in the country who was eligible to be appointed the chief of the commission and it is known that the person had to be persuaded to accept the position– the present chairperson. This is a weakness of the Act. This clause must be changed to say that the chief of the commission will work for five years, irrespective of age."[27]

Another significant feature relating to terms of appointment of the Chairperson and the members of the NHRC is that it debars the chairperson and the members from further employment under the Government of India or under the government of any state in India even after their retirement from the NHRC.[28] This is an extra-precaution to ensure the independence and impartiality of the chairperson and members of the NHRC.

To avoid any impediment in the regular and smooth working of the NHRC due to the occurrence of any vacancy in the office of the chairperson by reason of his / her death, resignation or otherwise, the Act has authorised the President to ask one of the members to act as the chairperson until the such vacancy is filled by regular appointment.[29] Similarly, when the chairperson is unable to discharge his / her functions owing to absence of leave or otherwise, the President may authorise by notification, any of its members to discharge the functions of the Chairperson until the date of which the chairperson resumes his / her duties.[30]

The salaries and allowances payable to, and other terms and conditions of service of the members of the NHRC are prescribed by rules made under the Act. It is further provided that neither the salary and allowances nor the other terms and conditions of service of a member shall be varied to his / her disadvantage after his / her appointment.[31] This has been done to ensure that NHRC does not act under any kind of government pressure and remains free from outside pressures.

Officers and Other Staff of the Commission

With regard to the other staff of NHRIs, the members should have the autonomy to select and appoint the staff but may, in appropriate cases, consult with the public service commission. Staff should be suitably qualified and sensitive to the NHRIs mandate. Staffing levels should be sufficient to adequately support the group of members in discharging the full mandate of the NHRI. An NHRI should ensure that its employment processes promote professionalism and equal employment opportunities.[32]

Besides the chairperson and the members, the NHRC consists of a Secretary-General, police and investigative, administrative, technical and scientific staff to support it in its effective functioning. As per the Act,[33] the Centrel Government shall make available an officer of the rank of Secretary to the Government of India to the NHRC to work as Secretary-General of the NHRC and also such police and investigative staff under an officer not below the rank of Director General of Police. To ensure independence of the NHRC, the 'say' of the NHRC should prevail in the appointment of the officials working under the NHRC and investigative staff should be made available as per the desire of the NHRC. However, the role of the government in making the rules governing the appointment and other service conditions of the staff of the NHRC puts a damper on the functional autonomy of the NHRC.

The NHRC has taken notice of this weakness of the Act and has made a recommendation to amend the Act so as to ensure the full functional autonomy of the NHRC. According to the amendment suggested by the NHRC:

'With a view to enhancing the credibility of the commission both within the country as well as outside, it is necessary that the Statute conveys a sense of the commission as being a truly autonomous body. Amendments to the statute should thus be so framed as to ensure this objective.

Thus, section 11(1)(b) should be so amended as to ensure that the opinion of the commission is determinant in the sanctioning and selection of officers and staff. It is, therefore, proposed that the words 'in the opinion of the commission' may be inserted after the word 'necessary' in line three of Section 11 (1)(b). Section 11(2) contemplates rules to be made by the Centrel Government in the matter of appointment of administrative, technical and scientific staff by the commission. It is suggested that the role of the government may be limited to the sanction of the required strength and matters such as appointment, postings, etc., may be left to the commission.'[34]

The amendments made by the NHRC in its very first annual report, which were repeated in its second and third report with a view to removing ambiguities and impediments concerning the competence of the NHRC. But action has not yet been taken to give effect to these recommendations for one or other reason.

Apart from this, another suggestion has been made regarding the recruitment of the staff of the NHRC with a view to enhance functional autonomy and professional efficiency of the NHRC. As per this suggestion, 'the staff of the commission should be men and women known for their impartiality and integrity; the composition of staff should reflect the pluralism and diversity of society, and ensure gender balance. Staff should be chosen from NGOs, minority groups, relevant professional groups and academics in order to enhance its credibility among all groups of society and impartiality in its functioning.'[35] But so far no action is taken in this direction by the government.

Functions of the NHRC

The objective of the NHRC is to promote, protect and secure human rights. The Paris Principles have advocated for granting NHRIs with 'as broad a mandate as possible' and entrusting all those functions which are deemed necessary for this purpose.[36] As per the Act, the NHRC is mandated to discharge the following functions :

(1) To inquire into the violation of human rights or abatement thereof, either on its own or on a petition submitted by an affected party or on his / her behalf by any person, or negligence shown by a public servant in the prevention of such a violation.

(2) To intervene in any of the proceedings pending before a court with the permission of such court or any complaint of violation of human rights.

(3) To visit any jail, or any other institution where persons are detained or lodged for purposes of treatment, reformation or protection under the control of a State Government with an advance notice to study the living conditions of the inmates and to make recommendations.

(4) To review the safeguards for the protection of human rights provided by the constitution or any of the existing law and to suggest measures to the Central and State Governments for their effective implementation.

(5) To review all the aspects that inhibit the enjoyment of human rights including the acts of terrorism and recommend the remedial measures to the Government.

(6) To study the treaties and other international instruments on human rights and make recommendations to the Central Government for their effective implementation.

(7) To undertake and promote research in the field of human rights.

(8) To propagate the concept of human rights and to promote the awareness for their protection among the various sections of the society, it can undertake publication of books or pamphlets or conduct seminars, or use the media or any other means available to it.

(9) To promote and support the non-governmental organisations and institutions working in the field of human rights.[37]

The broad range of functions assigned to the NHRC can be broadly categorised as : (1) Protective functions, (2) Monitoring Functions, (3) Advisory Functions, (4) Educational or Educative functions, and (5) Promotional functions.

Diagram No. 3.2

FUNCTIONS OF THE NHRC				
Protective Functions Section 12 (a) and (b)	Monitoring Functions Section 12 (c)	Advisory Functions Section 12 (d) (e) and (f)	Educational or Educative Functions Section 12 (g) and (h)	Promotional Functions Section 12 (f) and (g)

Protective Functions: Functions of the NHRC

Protective function is the first and foremost important task assigned to the NHRC. It relates to receiving complaints of human rights violations and initiating investigation into these complaints. Apparently, it appears very extensive power, but it is encircled with some reservations. The NHRC can only inquire into the complaint of violation of human rights or abetment thereof or negligence in the prevention of such violation by the 'public servants' only. It is to be noted that 'public servants are not the only persons who are violating human rights, but there are other violators, too, who indulge in human rights violations such as, land-lords, factory owners, contractors, terrorists, etc. The Act restricts the NHRC to look into the complaints of human rights violations against the public servants only.[38]

Leaving aside the above restrictive element in the protective functions of the NHRC, the other elements are in tune with the raw realities of the Indian human rights scenario. Interestingly, the NHRC can receive complaints or investigate on its own about 'negligence' in the prevention of human rights violations by public servants. It is pertinent to point out that this is particularly relevant provision since most of the human rights violations occur due to the non-performance of the statutory duties by the public servants.[39]

Another important aspect of the protective functions of the NHRC is its power to inquire *suo moto* into human rights violations. Its complementarity lies in its ability to 'search' for human rights violations. Two other crucial functions linked to its role as a protector are the power to intervene in legal proceedings that involve the violation of a fundamental rights[40] and the power of initiating new litigation.[41] In accepting complaints, the NHRC is required to confine its substantive consideration to those complaints that have been filed within one year of the perpetration of the alleged human rights violation.[42]

Monitoring Functions

Monitoring function of the NHRC is no less important. The Act authorises it to visit various custodial facilities in the country and monitor the state of affairs prevailing in these places from the viewpoint of custodial justice. Prisons, detention homes and states run welfare homes have sadly become seats of sadistic practices and theatre of torture and inhuman treatment of inmates. A large number of complaints relate to custodial violence, rape and torture. Thus, monitoring function becomes important from the point of view of enforcing systemic reforms relating to these custodial facilities.

However, there is some difficulty with this provision. The Act requires the NHRC to obtain the permission of the concerned state government prior to making its visit to these institutions.[43] This means that state governments are given an opportunity to improve the conditions in a given institution before such a visit and that as a result a true picture might not emerge. Furthermore, if detainees are interviewed in the presence of guards or other officials, it may not turn out to be useful exercise for the NHRC, because detainee may not come out with the real truth in the presence of institutional staff.

Another limitation of this provision is that it does not allow the NHRC or State Human Rights Commissions to investigate conditions in institutions under the control of the Centrel Government such as interrogation centres run by the armed forces (as these come within the jurisdiction of the Centrel Government). According to one suggestion, 'It is imperative that powers should be extended to ensure access to all places of detention[44] and international guidelines for the inspection of places of detention should be taken into account by the NHRC in drawing up guidelines for such visits.[45]

Despite the limitation of the provision given in the Act, the NHRC, disturbed by the increasing reports of violence in police lock-ups, took a decision that its officers would make surprise visits to police lock-ups. Accordingly, the Secretary General of the NHRC in a letter to the chief secretaries of the states /union territories on 1 August, 1997 requested them to issue necessary directions to the police authorities to enable officers of the NHRC to visit police lock-ups. Twenty-six states / union territories have since accepted this suggestion.[46]

The monitoring function of the NHRC has also come to the aid of the Supreme Court. The Supreme Court has assigned the NHRC the task of monitoring the administration of laws against the bonded labour and also monitoring the functioning of Mental Hospitals at Ranchi, Agra and Gwalior. The NHRC is also asked to overseeing the Agra Protection Home for Women.[47] Thus, the monitoring functions of the NHRC are of immense use in protecting and promoting human rights.

Advisory Functions

The NHRC is also assigned with the job of reviewing the constitutional safeguards and existing laws and making recommendations for appropriate amendments and measures to be taken for their effective implementation.[48] Although the Act does not explicitly confer power to the NHRC to draft new legislation, this authority flows by implication from the powers vested in the NHRC.[49] The NHRC's advisory functions include advising and assisting the government in the domestic implementation of international human rights standards by studying treaties and other international human rights instruments, recommending measures for their effective implementation and advising the ratification of a particular human rights instrument.[50]

In the course of the years, starting with its views on Terrorist and Disruptive Activities Act (TADA), the NHRC has reviewed and commented on some twenty Acts, Bills or Ordinances having human rights implications. These have related, interalia, to anti-terrorism legislation, the special powers of the armed forces, certain provisions of the Indian Penal Code and the Criminal Procedure Code, The police and prisons Acts, the rights of women and children, bonded labour, the rights of Dalits and Adivasis, issues relating to health and education, refugees, and the right to information.[51]

Educational and Educative Functions

Respect for the human rights of all, and the realisation of such rights, requires a continuous effort to evolve a culture that is sensitive to the basic needs of every human being, in a society that ensures equity and justice to every individual and every group. Human rights education is essential to the creation of such a culture and society.[52] A key statutory function assigned to the NHRC relates to the spread of human rights literacy among various sections of society.

The NHRC is acutely aware of the seriousness of the statutory responsibility enjoined upon it in this regard and has taken a number of steps to further human rights education.

These steps include :

- Working with the Ministry of Human Resources Development, The National Council for Educational Research and Training (NCERT) and the National Council for Teacher Education (NCTE) to prepare material for human rights education at all levels of schooling;
- Working with the University Grants Commission (UGC) for the development of human rights courses at the university level;
- Endowing a chair for Human Rights at the National Law School of India University in Bangalore;
- Encouraging courses on human rights in the training institutes for public servants, the police, para-military forces and army.
- Preparing a handbook of judicial officers;
- Offering a "Summer Internship Programme" for students, NGOs and professionals;
- Undertaking and sponsoring research projects in the field of human rights;
- Conducting and sponsoring conferences, seminars and workshops etc. on issues relating to human rights;
- Producing training material for staff of human rights commissions;
- Celebrating Human Rights Day, 50th Anniversary of the UDHR and other important international events relating to human rights;
- Publication of monthly bi-lingual newsletters, books and journal of the NHRC; and
- Utilising print and electronic media, films and documentaries to creative awareness and educate people about human rights issues.

Thus, educative functions of the NHRC focus on the long term strategy for the protection and promotion of human rights which is of primary importance in cultivating and nurturing the climate of human rights.

Promotional Functions

Corresponding to the educative functions, the Act requires the NHRC to encourage the efforts of non-governmental organisations and institutions active in the field of human rights. It also includes an umbrella clause under which the NHRC can perform such other functions as it may consider necessary for the promotion of human rights. The promotional functions add a pro-active role for the NHRC making it a convenient partner of the NGO community in the stupendous task of promotion of human rights awareness and literacy.

Recognising the work of non-governmental organisations as essential to the empowerment of the civil society, the NHRC encourages to promote networking amongst NGOs and itself. It also assists NGOs and others in organising programmes of relevance to human rights, providing modest financial support when appropriate. Just as the NHRC needs to turn to NGOs in every aspect of its work, so it has had to intercede on behalf of the NGOs – human rights defenders – when they experience harassment or difficulty. The NHRC supports and sponsors the representatives of the NGOs for human rights training programmes and helps in strengthening the capacity of NGOs through the training of their staff. The promotional functions of the NHRC include interaction with external groups and liasoning with international human rights bodies and fora etc.

Powers of the NHRC

As per the Paris Principles, an important power of an NHRI is its ability to protect the human rights of individuals by investigating violations and seeking remedies or redress for victims.[53] The NHRC is vested with broad powers relating to inquiries under the Act. These include :

- The NHRC exercises all of the powers of a Civil Court trying a suit under the Code of Civil Procedure, 1908, especially in respect to the procedure dealing with the examination of witnesses and evidence.
- The power to direct any person to submit such information as it may find useful or relevant to the matter under investigation. Such person is legally bound to furnish such information as directed by the NHRC within the meaning of Sections 176 and 177 of the Indian Penal Code.
- The power to search, seize and secure any document relating to the subject matter of inquiry by the NHRC or any other officer authorised by it subject to the provisions of Section 100 of the Code of Criminal Procedure, 1973 to the extent it may be applicable.
- Though empowered to exercise the powers of Civil Court only during the course of inquiring into the complaints, the NHRC has also the power to record the facts and the statement of an accused person as mentioned in Sections 175, 178, 179, 180 and 228 of the Indian Penal Code.
- The proceedings before the NHRC are deemed to be judicial proceedings within the meaning of Sections 193 and 228, and for the purposes of Section 196 of the Indian Penal Code, and also for the purposes of Section 195 and Chapter XXVI of the Code of Criminal Procedure, 1973.[54]

While in the course of inquiries, the NHRC has the powers of a civil court (set out in section 13 of the Act) including to summon attendance of witnesses, compel the provision of information and refer cases of contempt to a magistrate for initiation of contempt proceedings under the Code of Criminal Procedure, such powers are not given to the NHRC or individuals undertaking investigation on its behalf in the course of its activities beyond the conduct of inquiries, including when undertaking investigations.[55]

In the very first report of the NHRC, a recommendation for the amendment of the Section 13 (1) (f) of the Act was made with a view to removing ambiguities and impediments concerning the competence of the NHRC. As per the amendment suggested by the NHRC, Section 13 (1) (f) should be substituted by the following :

"Exercise the power to compel the attendance of any person to whom summons has been issued, under Section 32 of the Code."

And Also :

The existing Section 13 (1) (f) should be renumbered as Section 13 (1) (g).[56]

But no action has been taken to effect the suggested changes in the Act and the NHRC continues to suffer from the inherent weakness of the statute.

Investigative Powers

The NHRC exercises the following investigative powers while inquiring into the complaints of human rights violation :

- The power to utilise the services of any officer or any of the investigative agency of the Centrel or State Government with their prior approval.
- The officer or agency whose services are utilised by it shall be under the control and direction of the NHRC. Further, the NHRC may –

(a) summon and enforce the attendance of any person and examine him; or

(b) direct such person to discover or produce any document before it; or

(c) requisition any public record or copy therefrom from any office.

- Any statement made by a person before any officer or agency whose services are utilised or a statement made by a person in the course of giving evidence before the NHRC shall not be used against him in any civil or criminal proceedings; except for the purpose of prosecution for giving false evidence by such statement. However, the NHRC is empowered to use such statement if it is made in reply to a question asked by it or relevant to the subject matter of inquiry.

- If the NHRC is not satisfied about the correctness of the facts stated and any conclusion arrived at in the report submitted by such person, it may conduct an inquiry or examine such person or persons assisted the investigation.[57]
- If the NHRC at any stage of inquiry considers it necessary to inquire into the conduct of any person it may do so. But if in the opinion of the NHRC such an inquiry may prejudicially affect the reputation of the person, it has to give a reasonable opportunity to that person to produce evidence in his favour during such inquiry. However, the NHRC cannot conduct any inquiry if it affects the reputation of the person in any manner.[58]

The investigative powers vested in the NHRC by the Act are restrictive in nature and reflect negatively on the autonomy of the NHRC. The NHRC suffers from the lack of an independent investigation team and depend solely on the government bureaucracy as its investigation team has to be drawn essentially from the existing police personnel – provided by the Centrel or State Government – who are usually the human rights violators themselves. Moreover, by this restriction, the NHRC is unable to use the services of judicial officers, social workers, academicians and journalists.

Despite the statutory limitations as stated above, the experience of the NHRC's functioning repudiates the fears expressed by critics about the competence and independence of the NHRC concerning its investigative role. The NHRC has been fully aware of the misgivings in certain quarters as to whether the police and security apparatus of the country would cooperate with its investigating staff or whether investigating staff drawn essentially from the existing investigative agencies would be able to establish its own credentials of impartiality and fairness. In this regard, by its own admission, the NHRC has so far received total cooperation from the investigating staff and have been working in a fair and fearless way under the NHRC, receiving instructions from no other source but the commission.[59]

Investigation Procedure

The NHRC while inquiring into the complaints of violations of human rights adopts the following procedure :

- It can call for information or report either from the Central or any of the State Government concened or any other Authority, or organisation subordinate to them within the time frame fixed by it. However, it may proceed to inquire into the complaint on its own if it does not receive the information or report within the time frame. But, the NHRC shall not proceed further if it is satisfied upon the report submitted by the concerned Government or Authority along with the action initiated.

- If in the opinion of the NHRC, a matter requires immediate action, it can initiate inquiry even without asking the relevant Government or Authority for their report or information.[60]

Sometimes, the work of the NHRC has been hampered by delays in receiving reports from State authorities, often in cases which require the urgent attention of the NHRC.[61] Considering these problems, a suggestion has been made to empower the NHRC with legal authority to demand cooperation from government agencies – not just for the summoning of witnesses but to ensure that government agencies send prompt reports within the time-frame set down by the NHRC. One way to ensure this would be to give the NHRC the power to refer any person for prosecution who, without lawful excuse, obstructs the NHRC in the performance of its functions.[62] But the power to initiate inquiry into the complaints of human rights violations is not dependent on the government cooperation. Of course, it will definitely facilitate the process of inquiry.

Upon the completion of inquiry, the NHRC may take any of the following steps, namely :

- whether the inquiry discloses the violation of human rights or negligence in its prevention by a public servant, it may recommend to the concerned Government or Authority to take action against the concerned persons;
- approach the Supreme Court or High Court concerned to pass necessary orders;
- recommend to the concerned Government or Authority for grant of necessary interim relief to the victim or his family members;
- provide a copy of the inquiry report to the petitioner or his representative subject to the following provision.
- the NHRC shall send a copy of its inquiry report together with its recommendations to the concerned Government or Authority and it shall, within a month forward its comments to the NHRC on the report including the action taken or proposed to be taken by it.
- the NHRC shall publish its inquiry report together with the comments of the concerned Government or Authority, if any, and the action taken or proposed to be taken by the concerned Government or Authority on the recommendations of the NHRC.[63]

The Section 18 of the Act clearly gives only recommendatory powers to the NHRC which are termed as 'ineffective remedies for violation of human rights.'[64] In regard to the obligations of the governments, both Centrel and State, under Section 18 (5) of the Act, the NHRC's experience has not been happy. Barring honourable exceptions, concerned governments or authority have not bothered to send time-bound reports. The governments seem to be under the impression that the NHRC's deliberations are merely of a recommendatory value and not binding and thus, could be ignored.[65]

In order to enable the NHRC to have a greater say in the follow up action with a view to making an impact on the public mind on the effectiveness of the NHRC, an amendment of Section 18 has been recommended as follows :

For Sub-section (1), the existing text may be substituted by the following :

'Where the inquiry discloses the commission of violation of human rights or negligence in the prevention of violation of human rights by a public servant, it may initiate proceedings for prosecution or take such other action as the commission may deem fit against the concerned person/persons and award appropriate compensation.'

Sub-section (2) should be deleted.

Sub-section (3) may be rewarded as follows :

> 'Order the grant of such immediate interim relief to the victim or the members of his family as the commission may consider necessary, and as and when final compensation, if any, is determined in appropriate proceedings, interim compensation as may have been ordered, may be adjusted.'[66]

Again, no action has been taken to make the desired change in the statute and the NHRC's remedial powers remain non-binding.

Investigative Powers with Respect to Armed Forces

In regard to the complaints of violation of human rights committed by the members of the armed forces, the powers of the NHRC are quite limited. It can suo motu or on receipt of complaint may seek report from the Centrel Government. After receiving the report, the NHRC may drop proceedings or make recommendations to the Centrel Government. The NHRC has no powers of investigation into such complaints. The Centrel

Government is required to inform the NHRC of the action-taken on its recommendations within three months.[67]

Perhaps, this is the weakest clause in the whole of the statute governing the NHRC, reducing the potential effectiveness of the NHRC as a protector of human rights by virtually granting exemption to the armed forces from the NHRC's probe. In the words of a member of the NHRC, 'The present wording (of Section 19 and 19 (2)) has resulted in instances of a lack of accountability and, indeed, of opacity.'[68]

The NHRC itself has expressed concern about this limitation on several occasions, initially in its 1995-96 Annual Report. The 'Points for Consideration' also acknowledge that 'this exclusion has rendered a large number of violations by such personnel to go uninvestigated and unpunished.'[69] The more concerning is the rigidness of the position taken by the Government of India in this regard indicating no shift in the position as defined under the statute.

Despite this difficulty, the NHRC has chosen to construe Section 19 in such a way that the principal objects and reasons of the Act are served as constructively as possible. The NHRC has, thus, made clear to the Centrel Government that the power of the NHRC to make 'recommendations' under Section 19 must mean, as a corollary, that it has the power to do all that is necessary for the proper discharge of this responsibility. In the view of the NHRC, the 'report' that it seeks from the Centrel Government under Section 19 (1) must contain all the facts and occurrences relating to the alleged violation of human rights mentioned in the complaints; it must not merely be confined to the findings and conclusions reached by the Centrel Government on the basis of facts that are not disclosed to the NHRC. The NHRC has emphasised that only such a construction of Section 19 would promote the better protection of human rights in the country, which is the principal object of the Protection of Human Rights Act, 1993 and that such a construction must be preferred since it is in consonance with a settled canon relating to the interpretation of statutes. Thus, the determination of the NHRC to overcome the statutory hurdles and act in good faith with conviction and integrity holds it in good stride.

Moreover, apparently it may appear that the NHRC is powerless in respect of probing into the complaints of human rights violations committed by the members of the armed forces, but on a closer look, one can find that it is equipped with strategic weapon in the form of Section 19 (3) which enjoins the NHRC to publish its report along with its recommendations made to the Centrel Government and the action taken by the government. By publishing the report, the recommendations and response of the government, the public will come to know of the attitude of the government and the government will become accountable to the public. Hence, the NHRC can make government accountable in this respect.

Annual and Special Reports of the NHRC

The NHRC is required to submit an annual report to the Centrel Government and to the concerned state government and may at any time submit special reports on any matter which, in its opinion, is of such urgency or importance that it should not be deferred till submission of the annual report.

The Centrel and the State Government, in turn, would place these reports before the Parliament or the State Legislature together with the action taken report for discussion and debate.[71] Though these reports are of little consequence for the purpose of remedial powers, however, they are effective tools to educate public opinion as well as in determining the public accountability of the authorities concerned in the matters relating to human rights violations.

But, the NHRC is faced with the problem of the delays that occur in tabling the Annual Reports of the commission before the Parliament, together with the Memorandum of Action taken. And also, that there is virtually no debate in Parliament on the issues contained in the annual reports submitted by the NHRC, or the government's memoranda of action, when these are tabled.

The political apathy with which they are treated is clearly demonstrated by the fact that the Annual Report for 1996-1997 was not laid before Parliament (and thereby made public) until 9 months after its submission to the Centrel Government.

These delays have, in fact, amounted to a denial of the right to information of the people of the country. The NHRC has, therefore, recommended that Section 20 (2) of the Act be amended to ensure that the Annual Reports of the NHRC are placed before Parliament within a period of three months from the date of their receipt by the Centrel Government and that where the Report is not laid before Parliament within that period, it would be open to the NHRC to publish the Report.[72]

Complaints Handling Procedure

The complaint handling procedure is of great significance from the point of view of accessibility factor. That is why, it is essential that procedural aspects are to be clearly defined, legally entrenched and rigorously adhered to. The credibility of a national human rights institution depends to a great extent on the effective functioning of the complaint mechanism. The structure and functioning of the complaint mechanism should be such as to allow the national human rights institution to guarantee accessible, rapid and inexpensive resolution of a matter.[73]

In exercise of the powers conferred by Section 10 (2) of the Act, the NHRC has made the following regulations relating to the procedure for dealing with complaints :

(1) All complaints in whatever form received by the NHRC shall be registered and assigned a number and placed for admission before a Bench of two members constituted for the purpose.

(2) The complaints should be placed before the committee within a period of two weeks.

Ordinarily complaints of the following nature are not entertainable by the NHRC :

(a) In regard to events which happened more than a year before making of complaints;

(b) With regard to matters which are sub-judice;

(c) Which are vague, anonymous, pseudonymous;

(d) Which are of frivolous nature; or

(e) Those which are outside the purview of the NHRC.

(3) No fee is chargeable on complaints.

(4) Every attempt should be made to disclose a complete picture of the matter leading to the complaint. The complaint may be made in English or Hindi to enable the NHRC to take immediate action.

- To facilitate the filing of complaints, the NHRC shall entertain complaints in any language included in VII Schedule of the Constitution.

- It is open to the NHRC to ask for further information and affidavits to be filed in support of allegations what ever considered necessary.

(5) The NHRC may in its discretion accept telegraph complaints and complaints conveyed through fax.

(6) The NHRC shall have the power to dismiss the complaint *in limini.*

(7) Upon admission of a complaint, the Chairperson/Commission shall direct whether the matter would be set down for inquiry by it or should be investigated into.

(8) After the decision taken by the Chairperson/Commission on every complaint to either hold an inquiry or investigation, the Secretary shall ask for reports or comments from the concerned Government / Authority, giving a reasonable time to furnish the reports or comments.

(9) On receipt of the comments of the concerned Authority, a detailed note on the merits of the case shall be prepared for the consideration of the NHRC by the Secretariat.

(10) The directions and recommendations of the NHRC shall be communicated to the concerned Government / Authority and the petitioners as provided in Sections 18 and 19 of the Act.

(11) For the proper disposal of the matter, the NHRC has the discretion to give a personal hearing to the petitioner or any person on his behalf; call for records, cross-examine the witnesses; direct further investigation or undertake on the spot study.

The increase in the number of complaints received by the NHRC has necessitated drastic changes in its procedures for dealing with them. Apart from the constitution of single-member benches, certain other changes were also made in the procedures dealing with the complaints in order to make initial scrutiny more effective. The NHRC hired the services of the reputed management firm Mckinsey & Co. to undertake a study of its complaints handling procedures and suggest useful procedural innovations to strengthen the capability of the NHRC. Adjusting itself to the demand of fast increasing number of complaints, the NHRC has taken following measures :

- Computerisation of the entire caseload;
- Issuance of 'practice directions' on a wide variety of matters;
- 'Fast-tracking' of certain categories of complaints;
- 'Clubbing' together of similar complaints for procedural purposes;[75]
- recommended the constitution of District Police-Complaints Authority – to deal with police excesses and complaints at the district level – comprising of the Principal District Judge as Chairperson and the Collector and Senior Superintendent of Police as Members;[76] and
- suggested for the establishment of 'Human Rights Complaints Authorities.'

Yet, the problem of increasing case load remains a serious concern for the NHRC. The Act has envisaged that State Human Rights Commissions would share the burden of complaints with the NHRC. Therefore, steps should be taken to establish State Human Rights Commissions in all States as a matter of urgency.[77]

Jurisdiction of the NHRC

International guidelines prescribe, 'An NHRI should have a broad mandate covering full range of human rights issues and recognising the universality, interdependence, interrelatedness and indivisibility of human rights. 'Human rights' should be defined not only by reference to domestic law, but also by reference to all international human rights instruments, whether or not acceded to by the relevant state."[78]

But, as mentioned at the beginning of this chapter, the Act has defined the term 'human rights' in a narrow sense and thereby restricting the scope of jurisdiction of the NHRC and putting a rider on the meaning of the term 'International Covenants' as well.

Similarly, the term 'armed forces' as defined in the Act, means the naval, military and air forces and includes any other armed forces of the Union.[79] The implication of this definition is that even the paramilitary forces are excluded from the purview of inquiry by the NHRC as under Section 19, the NHRC has got the power to seek report from the Centrel Government on violation of human rights committed by the security forces and make recommendations to the government. It cannot undertake any inquiry by itself as in other cases. Thus, Section 2(1)(a) and Section 19 virtually end up in keeping the armed forces and paramilitary forces outside the NHRC's power of investigation and limits the jurisdiction of the NHRC.

State Human Rights Commissions have even less powers in relation to armed forces than the NHRC, making their position within states, where the majority of allegations of human rights violations are against the members of the armed forces, almost untenable. This has led to the chair of the Assam Human Rights Commission recommending that the Protection of Human Rights Act be amended so that the state commission can investigate allegations of human rights violations by the members of the armed forces.[80]

Another provision under the Act having negative effect on the jurisdiction of the NHRC is Section 1(2) relating to the role of the NHRC in respect of the State of Jammu and Kashmir. It implies the restriction of the powers of the NHRC with respect to matters relating to public order, police, prisons, etc. (covered in List II of the Seventh Schedule of the Constitution) in Jammu and Kashmir.[81] Thus, the Act has limited applicability for the State of Jammu and Kashmir due to the special constitutional status granted to the state.

Similarly, Section 2(2) of the Act, too, points to the restrictive approach of the statute with respect to the jurisdiction of the NHRC, confining the provision to the State of Jammu and Kashmir. The NHRC has suggested to amend the provision with a view to broad base it to cover any such contingency in any area instead of the provision being restricted to the State of Jammu and Kashmir.[82]

One more clause explicitly keeps a specified type of cases outside the jurisdiction of the NHRC. Section 36 (1) of the Act states that the NHRC should not inquire into any matter pending before a State Human Rights Commission or any other commission duly constituted under any law for the time being in force.

The experience of the NHRC has shown that Section 36 of the Act, dealing with 'matters not subject to the jurisdiction of the commission' has lent itself to efforts to thwart the purposes of the Act. On occasion, this has been done by bringing a matter before a State Human Rights Commission or some other commission in similar or slightly modified manner, in order to seek to block the jurisdiction of the NHRC. On other occasions, this has been done by setting-up a commission under the Commission of Inquiries Act, after the NHRC has also taken cognizance of a matter, and then questioning the jurisdiction of the NHRC, in a court of law, to proceed with its efforts or monitor a situation.[83]

Another sub-clause of the Section 36 puts further restriction on the jurisdiction of the NHRC by placing a time-limit of one year after which the NHRC cannot take cognizance of a complaint. This provision obstructs the path of justice in deserving cases where for any reason, the one year limiting stipulation could not be adhered to.[84]

Despite these statutory blocks on the jurisdiction of the NHRC, the Supreme Court's actions, reposing full faith in the NHRC's competence, tantamounts to the extension of ambit of jurisdiction of the NHRC. In the infamous 'Punjab Mass Cremation Case', the Supreme Court, on 12th December, 1996 referred the matter to the NHRC to determine all issues arising from the case. Although, the NHRC's jurisdiction came in for question under the Section 36 (2) of the Act, but the explanation given by the NHRC in this regard said that the Supreme Court had designated the NHRC as a body *sui generis* to carry out functions and determine issues as entrusted to it by the Court. 'The shackles and limitations under the Act are not attracted to this body as, indeed, it does not function under the provisions of the Act but under the remit of the Supreme Court. The Court made the order in exercise of the plenitude of its jurisdiction under Article 32 of the Constitution. That, for the parties and NHRC, has the effect and force of law. The expression 'to have the matter examined in accordance with law' is not necessarily the same thing as 'to function strictly within the limitation of the Act.' The Supreme Court referred the matter to the NHRC for the protection of human rights. As a logical consequence, the powers of the NHRC in carrying out this mandate are not limited by Section 36 (2) or other limiting provisions of the Act.[85]

NHRC and State Human Rights Commissions

A country of the size and diversity of India cannot be catered by a centralised organisation, specially in the matter of protection and promotion of human rights. Human Rights Commissions at the State level are needed for obvious reasons, such as, the redressal of grievances needed to be swift and inexpensive; the message of human rights must reach the grass-root level in the languages of the people of the country; the federal character of our constitution must be respected; the nation-wide challenge needs an army of activists in each state and in each district, if societal and attitudinal changes are to be brought. The Protection of Human Rights Act, 1993 was prescient in envisaging the need for State Human Rights Commissions,[86] and provided, under the Chapter V, the decentralised structure constituted along the same lines as that of the NHRC and with the same functions in theory as that of the NHRC.

However, there is a flaw in the language of the provision given in the Act which makes the establishment of the State Human Rights Commissions as optional for the state. Section 21(1) states that 'A State Government may constitute a body known as the 'State's Human Rights Commission' whereas Section 3 (1) of the Act states that the Central Government shall constitute a body to be known as the National Human Rights Commission. For establishing the State Human Rights Commission, the word used is 'may' but for establishing National Human Rights Commission, the word is used 'shall'. Meaning thereby, that Section 3 (1) makes it mandatory to constitute NHRC for the Centrel Government while in the case of State Human Rights Commissions, it is merely recommendatory provision for the state governments.[87]

Considering the above fact, the NHRC has been advising states, both through letters to their chief ministers and through discussions with them, to set-up state commissions as envisaged in the Act,[88] at the earliest. There has been positive response from some of the states, but majority of them are still without State Human Rights Commissions.[89]

While it is most desirable that state-level commissions be established rapidly, certain state governments have informed the NHRC of their difficulty in proceeding with it because of the financial constraints or because of the non-availability of retired Chief Justice or Justices of the High Court whose presence is essential to the proper composition of the five-member commissions envisaged under the provisions of Section 21(2) of the Act. As these difficulties cannot be willed away particularly in respect of the states in the North-Eastern region where there is a single High Court based in Guwahati, a formula may need to be especially devised for these states in respect of Human Rights Commissions.[90]

Having carefully considered various options in respect of the seven North-Eastern states, the NHRC wrote to the chief ministers of those states, suggesting the setting up of a separate Human Rights Commission or each state, having a core comprising the chairperson and the judicial member of the Assam Human Rights Commission, who would act as members of the state commission in each of the other states, along with one human rights activist nominated by that state. As an alternative model, the NHRC pointed out that there could be a common commission for the states of North-East, with individual states contributing to the establishment. However, both these options would entail appropriate amendment to the Act.[91] The NHRC has also recommended that this issue should receive the attention of the Centrel Government and the leadership of political parties at the highest level.

The Protection of Human Rights Act, 1993 provides for a National Human Rights Commission and State Human Rights Commissions. But there is no specific mention in the statute on the setting-up of commissions at the level of union territories. The presumption could be that the commission at the national level will serve the union territories as well. However, this militates against the concept of a decentralised grievance redressal machinery through state commissions. The NHRC, therefore, is of the view that the union territories as well as the National Capital Territory of Delhi should have their own arrangements for the discharge of certain of the responsibilities specified in the Act. The NHRC has accordingly recommended that the Government of India take steps for evolving suitable institutional mechanism for the protection and promotion of human rights in Union Territories including the National Territory of Delhi.[92]

The statute fails to define the relationship between the NHRC and the State Human Rights Commissions in clear terms. With the increase in the number of State Human Rights Commissions, it is important than ever before to ensure that their work is carefully coordinated with that of the NHRC and that confusion and duplication does not occur. Under Section 21(5) of the Act, a state commission 'may inquire into violation of human rights only in respect of matters relatable to any of the entries enumerated in List II and List III in the Seventh Schedule to the Constitution.' Further, Section 36 (1) of the Act, states that the National Human Rights Commission 'shall not inquire into any matter which is pending before a State Commission or any other Commission duly constituted under any law for the time being in force.'[93]

With a view to establishing a clear and harmonious functional relationship between the National Human Rights Commission and State Human Rights Commissions, the NHRC had recommended the following amendment to Section 36 (1) of the Protection of Human Rights Act, 1993:

At the end of sub-section (2), the following may be added :

'Provided that the Commission may entertain a matter for inquiry beyond a year if it is satisfied that the delay is explained to its satisfaction.'

(3) 'The State Commission shall be subject to the judicial control of the Commission and the State Commission's orders and directions would be open to challenge before the Commission by way of revision.'[94]

But, as is the case with other suggested amendments, this too is not acted upon by the government. In the meantime, however, in order to ensure proper coordination in the work of the NHRC and State Human Rights Commissions and also to avoid duplication, exchanges of information on a fortnightly basis have been instituted in respect of the cases of which cognizance has been taken by the NHRC and state commisions.[95]

Thus, the NHRC has encouraged the establishment of the State Human Rights Commissions and is eager to share its burden of excessive number of grievances against human rights violations, together with extending all kinds of help to strengthen their capability to work for the protection and promotion of human rights on a regular basis.

NHRC and Human Rights Courts

The Protection of Human Rights Act, 1993 provides for the establishment of 'Human Rights Courts' to provide 'speedy trial of offences arising out of violation of human rights.' Section 30 provides the power of the state government to specify for each district a Court of Sessions to be a Human Rights Court for the trial of offences arising out of violation of human rights with the concurrence of the Chief Justice of the High Court, by notification.

Several state governments– including Andhra Pradesh, Assam, Sikkim, Tamil Nadu and Uttar Pradesh – have notified the setting up of human rights courts by designating sessions courts to hear human rights cases. However, in Tamil Nadu, the process was challenged by officials of the courts themselves and human rights activists who pointed to the fact that there are no guidelines as to the mandate and powers of these courts or the procedures which the courts should follow. The Tamil Nadu High Court gave an order in this regard in June 1997.

The High Court of Madras, touching on the interpretation of various provisions of the Protection of Human Rights Act, 1993, gave its views on the various aspects of the functioning of Human Rights Courts. It pointed out that Human Rights Court was not a Court or Tribunal of a Court constituted under Article 323-A or 323-B of the Constitution, but it was a Court constituted under Section 30 of the Act, as a 'Special Court' in the cadre of a Court of Session with powers of a Court of original jurisdiction for trial of all offences arising out of violation of human rights, irrespective of their classification into various categories of offences – First class, Second class or exclusively triable by Court of Session is permissible under law. Further, it reiterated that the scheme of the Protection of Human Rights Act in constituting NHRC, SHRC and HRC indicated, in no uncertain terms, the NHRC and SHRC were akin to the Commission of Inquiry set-up under Commission of Inquiry Act and had no powers to give a definitive judgement in respect of offences arising out of violation of human rights and were constituted with the object of creating awareness of human rights at the governmental level and the public at large excepting the fact they were permanent Standing Commissions, while in sharp contrast, the only institution which can inquire into, adjudicate upon and punish for violation of human rights is Human Rights Court – first of its kind, anywhere in the world.[96]

No doubt, Human Rights Courts are indigenous innovation introduced by the Protection of Human Rights Act, 1993, however, it remains an idle device in the absence of certain desirable rectifications such as :

- Human Rights Courts must have to be invested with the exclusive jurisdiction in the matter of award of compensation to the victims of human rights offences;[97]
- The requirement for governmental sanction for the prosecution of public servants should be removed in cases brought before human rights courts;
- An effective system for the provision of legal aid should accompany the establishment of human rights courts;
- The NHRC or SHRC should ensure the training and sensitization in international human rights standards of judiciary and prosecutors engaged in hearing cases of human rights courts;
- Separate and adequate resources should be allocated to the functioning of human rights courts.[98]

Apart from the statutory provision for the establishment of human rights courts at the district level, another innovative step was taken by Kerala with the creation of District Level Committees as a further means of decentralisation of the process of the redressal of human rights grievances and speedy and sensitively handled disposal of complaints at the local level. Kerala's example has been followed in Andhra Pradesh and also in Chandigarh and the Andaman and Nicobar Islands. The NHRC has recommended for the establishment of District Level Committee in other states and union territories as well.[99]

For the purpose of the speedier disposal of the complaints and to act preventively, in all regions of the country, the NHRC has been examining ways in which it can best decentralise its own administrative machinery through regional offices or circuit benches of the NHRC.[100]

NHRC and the Supreme Court

As far as the relationship of the NHRC with Supreme Court is concerned, it has been stated that 'National Human Rights Institutions like the NHRC in India should in no way operate in the absence of, as a substitute for, other fundamental social, legal or judicial infrastructure.'[101] The NHRI's should play a role complementary to that of courts. The NHRIs should be accorded standing to bring complaints to courts in their own right. Courts should accord NHRIs official status as a friend of the court. Courts should grant to NHRIs the rights to join as a party in relevant cases. The NHRIs should try to establish a cooperative working relationship with the courts.[102]

In the light of the above defined relationship of NHRIs with the judiciary, the Protection of Human Rights Act, 1993, provides for the NHRC to 'intervene in any proceedings involving any allegation of violation of human rights pending before a court with the approval of such court.'[103] The Act further empowers the NHRC to 'approach the Supreme Court or the High Court concerned for such directions, orders or writs as that court may deem necessary.'[104]

The NHRC has approached the courts in several cases to protect human rights of the vulnerable people including in pending cases. One such case related to the Chakma refugees in Arunachal Pradesh where the NHRC decided to approach the Supreme Court through a writ petition seeking to enforce the right to life of about 65,000 Chakma/Hajong refugees who were facing forcible eviction from the state despite the NHRC's directives to the contrary.

The Supreme Court held that Chakmas shall not be evicted from their homes and shall not be denied life and comfort therein, except in accordance with law.[105] The NHRC also took a decision to seek to be impleaded in the proceedings pending before the Supreme Court in respect of the Armed Forces (Special Powers) Act, 1958 and to assist the court by placing the NHRC's views before it on the issues that had arisen in that connection.[106] Thus, the NHRC has been involved in a number of cases relating of protection of human rights pending before the Supreme Court.

The Supreme Court, on its part, has itself remitted to the NHRC certain complex issues, having serious human rights implications. These included :

- The grave and persistent problem of bonded labour in the country;
- The recurrent allegations of starvation deaths in the Koraput – Bolangir – Kalahandi districts of Orissa;
- The proper running of institutions located at Agra, Gwalior and Ranchi for persons with mental disabilities;
- The proper running of the Protective Home for women in Agra.[107]

Hence, the NHRC plays a role complementary to that of the superior courts of the country in the defense of human rights and constitutional guarantees, a role that has often been described as symbiotic.[108]

Complimentarity between the judiciary and the NHRC has been of great advantage in so far as the role of the NHRC for protecting human rights is concerned.[109]

Financial Autonomy of the NHRC

The Paris Principles call for 'adequate funding' for a National Human Rights Institution so as to insulate it from governmental financial control.[110] The Protection of Human Rights Act, 1993 provides, "The Central Government shall after due appropriation made by Parliament by law in this behalf, pay to the Commission by way of grants such sum of money as the Central Government may think fit for being utilised for the purposes of this Act."[111] As per this provision, the NHRC does not have substantial financial autonomy. Although, it receives Parliament approved grants, the actual amount it is paid is, however, decided by the government. Nevertheless, the NHRC enjoys the freedom to spend the money granted as it thinks fit for performing the functions under the Act.[112]

For some analysts, funding through parliament as opposed to a particular ministry has certain in-built checks in that the opposition parties (in Parliament) can expose and / or thwart the government's attempts to starve the NHRC. Also, this method ensures a greater degree of functional autonomy to the commission.[113] But the Annual Report of the NHRC for 1996-97 refers to some of the difficulties that the NHRC has been facing in conducting the research it considers necessary, using the expertise of organisations and institutions with which the NHRC has contact.

The Planning Commission of India offered a grant of Rupees Twenty-five lacs to the NHRC for specific areas of research on the basis that the NHRC would not provide grants to other institutions to undertake any of this research. The NHRC, therefore, refused the grant indicating that it would find the funds elsewhere.[114]

To overcome these difficulties, the NHRC requires greater financial autonomy, adequate resource allocation secured with a long-term perspective, right to draft its own budget and free from the financial control of the government. Then only, it will be able to carry out its mandated functions to hilt.

Organisational Structure of the Secretariat

Diagram No. 33

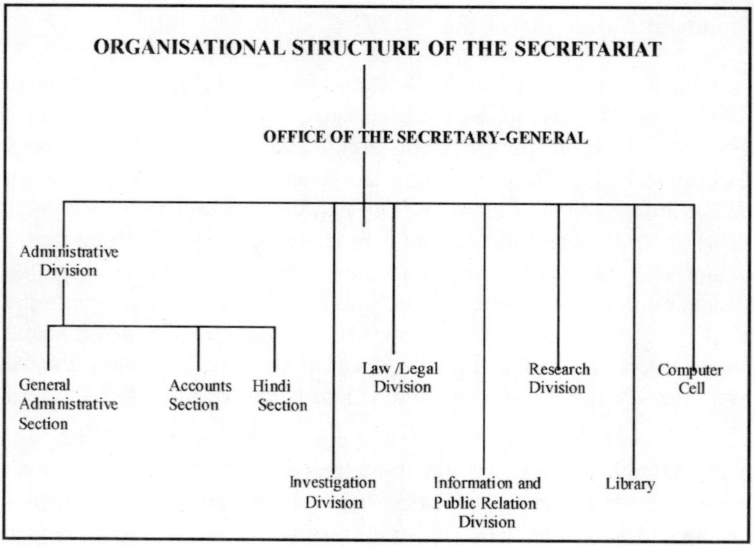

Organisation of NHRC's Secretariat and its Working

As far as the Secretariat of the NHRC is concerned, the Act provides, 'There shall be a Secretary-General who shall be the Chief Executive Officer of the Commission and shall exercise such power and discharge such functions of the Commission as it may delegate to him.'[115] Further, the Act states, 'The Central Government shall make available to the Commission : (a) an officer of the rank of the Secretary to the Government of India who shall be the Secretary General of the Commission.'[116] The Act also authorises the NHRC to appoint such other administrative, technical and scientific staff as it may consider necessary, subject to such rules as may be made by the Centrel Government in this behalf. Salaries, allowances and conditions of service of the officers and other staff appointed by the NHRC shall be such as may be prescribed.[17]

The Act does not say much about the constitution of the Secretariat of the NHRC and the method of recruitment of the staff, allowing functional autonomy to the NHRC. The NHRC is empowered to regulate its own procedure. However, the salaries, allowances and service conditions are regulated by the Central Government. Similarly, the Act makes a provision for the Secretary-General and the Director (Investigation) only; rest of the staff is left to the discretion of the NHRC with no fixed strength. However, appointments for the additional posts need prior sanction from the Home and Finance Ministries. The NHRC has not yet formed its own cadre. Therefore, it has adopted different ways of recruitment which include deputation, contract and direct recruitment. The shape and size of the Secretariat of the NHRC is passing through the formative phase. Hence, it is growing gradually as per its needs.[118] In this task, the Secretariat of the NHRC is led by the Secretary-General.

Secretary General of the NHRC

As per the Act, the Secretary-General is the Chief Executive Officer (CEO) of the NHRC. As its administrative head, he manages the affairs of the Secretariat and is directly responsible to the NHRC. All orders and decisions of the NHRC are authenticated by him. His duties include coordinating the working of different divisions and departments of the Secretariat and maintaining liaison with various ministries of the Government of India. He also represents the NHRC on different fora and seminars, etc. He supervises the smooth functioning of the Secretariat in handling complaints, planning investigations, conveying guidelines, conducting studies and research projects and handling communications, etc. He has an important role to play in enhancing the credibility of the NHRC.

The Secretariat of the NHRC comprises mainly five divisions. They include Administrative Division, Investigation Division, Information and Public Relation Division, Legal or Law Division and Research Division. Of these five divisions, the first two divisions get mention in the Act. Rest of these divisions came into being as per the need of the task assigned to the NHRC. Besides these divisions, the Secretariat maintains a rich-resource library and a computer cell as well[119] (Diagram No. 3.3).

Administrative Division

Administrative Division consists of three sections, namely, General Administration Section, Accounts Section and Hindi-Section. This division deals with all administrative, personnel, establishment, cadre matters of all the staff and officers of the NHRC. It is headed by a Joint-Secretary who is associated by a Director, two Under-Secretaries, two Section-officers and other ministerial staff.

The tasks of this division include arranging the meetings of the full commission, daily-meetings of the commission and issuing notices and agenda for these meetings. It also takes care of planning the visits / tours of the NHRC members and officials both within the country and foreign tours. It also looks after the Protocol, arranging staff identity cards and logistics for the NHRC.

General Administration Section

The General Administration Section under the Administrative Division, performs basically all the housekeeping tasks such as supplying stationery, furniture, office-equipments and various other items of need to different divisions and staff. It is also entrusted with the maintenance, renovation and repairs etc. of the workplace and also of the residences allotted to the Chairperson and other members of the NHRC by keeping close liaison with the C.P.W.D. This Section is headed by the Under-Secretary (Estt.) and is assisted by a Drawing and Disbursing Officer (DDO).

Accounts Section

The Accounts Section maintains the accounts of the NHRC, prepares budget and looks after all the financial matters of the NHRC. The section is headed by a Joint-Secretary and the staff under him includes one Senior Accounts Officer, three Assistant Accounts Officers and other ministerial employees.

Hindi Section

Considering the fact that a large number of complaints were received by the NHRC in Hindi, it was decided to have a Hindi cell in the Secretariat. Therefore, the Hindi Section was established in 1996. This cell, apart from working towards compliance with the provisions of the Official Language Act, helps with the translation of complaints received in other Indian languages.

It also takes care of Monthly Newsletter and Annual Reports of the NHRC which are published in Hindi also. It has also introduced correspondence in Hindi in the Secretariat.[120]

Investigation Division

The Investigation Division is one of the most important department of the Secretariat as it investigates into the complaints either through its own initiative or in response to a petition filed by a person relating to human rights violations. The importance of this division is indicated by the fact that the provision for it is made in the Act. As per the Act, the Investigation Division is being headed by an officer of the rank of Director-General of Police who is appointed by the NHRC.[121] Rule 18 of the NHRC's Procedural Regulations lays down that the investigation staff will, in addition to a Director General, consists of the Deputy Inspector-General of Police, two Superintendent of Police, six Deputy Superintendents of Police, twenty-four Inspectors of Police and such other categories of officers as the NHRC from time to time decides. Further under Rule 18, the NHRC may, in any given case, appoint an appropriate number of outsiders to be associated with the investigation either as Investigators or observers (Diagram No. 3.4). As of 31st March, 1997, the Investigation Division had a staff of 83 persons.

Diagram No. 3.4 : Investigation Division

INVESTIGATION DIVISION

DIRECTOR – GENERAL (INVESTIGATION)

↓

DEPUTY INSPECTOR GENERAL (DIG)

↓

SENIOR SUPERINTENDENT OF POLICE (SSP)

↓

SUPERINTENDENT OF POLICE (SP)

↓

DEPUTY SUPERINTENDENT OF POLICE (DSP)

↓

INSPECTOR OF POLICE

As the head of the Division, the Director General is responsible for the whole process of investigation into complaints of human rights violation. The process of investigation must comply the Act which enjoins wide powers of investigation, examination of witnesses, and preparing inquiry report to be submitted to the NHRC for making its own recommendations etc.

Besides undertaking investigative tasks, this division also sends delegations on fact-finding missions to gather more information about incidents of human rights violations. For example a delegation has been sent to Jammu and Kashmir for an on the spot study to acquaint with the facts of ground situation. These are the main responsibilities of the division with the hierarchy of functioning.[122]

Legal or Law Division

Another important division of the Secretariat which plays the central role in both receiving of complaints and redressal procedure of such complaints is the Legal or Law Division. It keeps informed the petitioner and the opposite party about the action-taken or likely to be taken in that regard. This division is entrusted with the responsibility of handling the complaints at various stages and keep a record of the status of the complaint. It is faced with a burdensome job, but its functioning is quite systematic and meticulous. For the better management of the tasks assigned to it, the NHRC made use of the professional management advisory services of a famous foreign consultancy firm and adopted computerizational functioning to increase its efficiency.

This division is led by a Registrar, one Joint-Registrar, one Deputy-Registrar, five Assistant Registrars, Six Section-Officers, nine Office Assistants and ministerial staff. Besides, dealing with the complaints, this division is also called upon to impart training to other departments of the Secretariat and outside organisations / institutions as well.

Information and Public Relation Division

At the time of the inception, the NHRC sent a proposal about the different departments required under the Secretariat besides the approved general administration, investigation and Law/legal divisions. The said proposal included Information and Public Relation Division as important component of the Secretariat to play the role of educator of public opinion which is very necessary for the protection and promotion of human rights.[123]

As a consequence to the proposal made by the NHRC, the Information and Public Relation Division was established under the Secretariat in 1994-95. This division makes a valuable contribution to the dissemination of information on the work carried out by the NHRC, using both the print and electronic media. It is also responsible for the organisation of press conferences and briefings and issuance of press-releases.[124] Besides, it also maintains a data-base entitled Newspaper Clipping Information System (NPCIS), concerning certain important features of press reactions to NHRC's work. It also establishes coordination with NGOs. This division is also responsible for the production and distribution of pamphlets/ brochures/audio-spots and video-spots on human rights. It is headed by an Information and Public Relation Officer who also acts as the Editor of the monthly Human Rights Newsletter, Annual Reports and other editorial matters of the NHRC.[125]

Research Division

Another division that found mention in the proposal sent by the NHRC regarding the expansion of the Secretariat was the Research Division. Although, the said proposal for the establishment of the Research Division was made in the very first annual report of the NHRC, but it could not start functioning until 1996 due to the non-availability of a qualified person as desired by the NHRC to lead this division and also due to the lack of funds.[126] Finally, Planning Commission agreed to provide grants for research activities of the NHRC. However, the NHRC has to face some technical obstructions with Planning Commission in the matter of funding of research projects. This led to the restructuring of the Research Division and converting it into a Policy, Research, Projects and Programmes Division (PRPPD) for the purpose of rationalising its on-going projects and programmes with a view to ensuring that greater coherence and consistency were brought to bear on them and a sense of priority was established and respected.[127]

The Policy, Research, Projects and Programme Division is headed by a Director (Research). It works in close cooperation with the Law Division and gives advice on research matters to the members of the NHRC. This division undertakes research projects on its own on the subjects relating to human rights issues. It also sponsors research projects of outside institutions including colleges, universities and non governmental organisations.

Library

Besides the five above mentioned divisions, the Secretariat has established its own library-cum-documentation centre which is very useful to the NHRC, interns and scholars engaged in research relating to human rights. It maintains a rich collection of books, journals, periodicals, key-legal publications, UN documents and NGO's reports plus NHRC's own publications etc., having relevance to its functions. The library is also receiving books from abroad, as well as from various ministries/ departments of the Government of India.

Computer Cell

In view of the large number of complaints that the NHRC had been receiving right from the time of its inception, the NHRC thought it essential to go for a comprehensive programme of computerisation to facilitate efficient disposal of complaints and to establish the communication network with the State capitals as also the districts.

In close collaboration with the National Informatic Centre (NIC), it has developed a user-friendly software for monitoring the status of complaints, from receipt to final disposal. This is of great help to the Law Division. The facility has also been undertaken to update the case record, so that, at any point of time, the status of any complaint can be assessed by the members and the officers of the NHRC. Now, the management information system and library is also computerised. This cell has contributed a lot in making NHRC technology-savy organisation.

The NHRC, as an institution of good governance, constantly aspires and seeks to function with the highest standards of efficiency and integrity. In the face of exceptional new challenges, it has worked upon to tighten and strengthen its methods of working in order to prove worthy of the trust and expectations reposed in it. The efficient working of the Secretariat is the biggest strength of the NHRC.

References

1. Quoted in "Evolution of the National Human Rights Commission, 1993-2002 : A Decennial Review" by Virendra Dayal, *Journal of the NHRC*, Vol. 1 (2002), p. 41.
2. Section 3, section 21 and section 30 of the Protection of Human Rights Act, 1993 (Hereinafter, it is referred as the Act).
3. Section 2 (1) (d).

4. *Ibid.*, Section 2 (1) (f).
5. T. Suryanarayana Sastry, "The Structure, Functions and Powers of the National Human Rights Commission of India," *Indian Journal of International Law*, Vol. 37 (1), Jan.-March 1997, pp. 102-103.
6. *Annual Report of the NHRC* (1993-94), para 13.3, p. 34. Also see, annexure – VI attached to the *Annual Report* (1993-94), p. 50.
7. *Ibid.*
8. *Vishaka Vs. State of Rajasthan* (1997) 6 SC 241.
9. Section 3 (2) (3) and (4) of the Act.
10. National Human Rights Institutions : Best Practices, Commonwealth Secretariat, (London : 2001), p. 14.
11. Mangari Rajendar, "*The Protection of Human Rights Act, 1993 and Relating Laws*", (Hyderabad : 2000), p.13.
12. UN Handbook on the Establishment and Strengthening of National Institutions for the Promotion and Protection of Human Rights, (United Nations, Geneva, 1995) (Hereinafter UN Handbook), p.12.
13. Vijayashri Sripati, "India's National Human Rights Commission : Strengths and Weaknesses" in *National Human Rights Institutions* (eds.) Lindsnaes, Lindholt and Yigen, (Danish Center for Human Rights : 2000), p. 155.
14. Supra no. 10, p. 16.
15. Section 4 (1) of the Act.
16. *Ibid.*
17. Kuldeep Nayar, "Human Rights Diary", *Hindu* (Madras) 27 November, 1999.
18. *Ibid.*
19. A.G. Noorani, "Rites of Life – II : Commission of Force or Fraud?" in *Statesman* (New Delhi), 2 June, 1993.
20. *Ibid.*
21. Supra no. 11, pp. 14-15.
22. Supra no. 10, f.n. 2, p. 16.
23. Supra no. 12, para 2.3.
24. Section 5 (1) of the Act.
25. Section 5 (2) of the Act.
26. Supra no. 12, pp. 16-17.

27. Y.P. Chhibar, "National Human Rights Commission : A View from People's Front" in "*Human Rights : Fifty Years of India's Independence*". (ed.) K.P. Saksena, (New Delhi : 1999), p. 121.
28. Section 6 (3) of the Act.
29. Section 7 (1) of the Act.
30. Section 7 (2) of the Act.
31. Section 8 of the Act.
32. Supra no. 10, p. 13-14.
33. Section 11 (1), 11 (2) and 11(3) of the Act.
34. See, annexure no. VI to the Annual Report of the NHRC (1993-94), p. 50.
35. Summary of the Submission to the Advisory Committee of the Amnesty International (India) established to review provisions of the Protection of Human Rights Act, 1993, AI Index : ASA 20/26/98, October 1998, pp. 17-18.
36. Supra no 10, pp. 18-20.
37. Section 12 of the Act.
38. Supra 11, p. 21.
39. Supra no. 13, p. 158.
40. Section 12 (b) of the Act.
41. Section 18 (2) of the Act.
42. Section 36 (2) of the Act.
43. Section 12 (c) of the Act.
44. Supra no. 35, p. 19
45. International Committee of Red Cross (ICRC) statement to the 48th session of the UN Human Rights Commission under Point 10 (detention) 12 February 1992; and also Amnesty International's report, "The Draft Optional Protocol to the Convention Against Torture : Developing an effective Tool to prevent Torture", July 1996, AI Index : IOR 51/01/96.
46. Annual Report of the NHRC, (1997-98), para no. 3.26.
47. Annual Report of the NHRC, (1998-99), Annexure-I, pp. 105-107.
48. Section 12 (d) of the Act.
49. Annual Report of the NHRC, (1995-96), p. 24.
50. Section 12 (f) of the Act.
51. Virendra Dayal, Op.cit., pp. 66-67.

52. Annual Report of the NHRC, (1999-2000), para no. 12.1, p. 67.
53. Supra no. 10, p. 21.
54. Section 13 of the Act.
55. Report of Amnesty International, supra no. 35, p. 8.
56. Annual Report of the NHRC (1993-94), Annexure No. VI, p. 51.
57. Sections 14 and 15 of the Act.
58. Section 16 of the Act.
59. Annual Report of the NHRC (1995-96) para no. 9.14, pp. 46-47.
60. Section 17 of the Act.
61. One of the first directives of the NHRC after its establishment was to request all state governments to report incidences of deaths in custody or custodial rape to the NHRC within 24 hours. Failure to provide prompt report would give rise to the presumption that there was an attempt to suppress the incident. Some states have sent regular reports to the NHRC while some others have not done so.
62. Report of the Amnesty International, supra no. 35, pp. 8-9.
63. Section 18 of the Act.
64. Vijayshri Sripati, op. cit., p.161.
65. 'Points for Consideration' sent by the Advisory Committee under the Chairmanship of Hon'ble Mr Justice A.M. Ahmadi on the amendments to the Protection of Human Rights Act, 1993, para no. 2.8.
66. Annual Report of the NHRC (1993-94), Annexure No. VI, p. 51.
67. Section 19 of the Act.
68. Virendra Dayal, op. cit. p. 45.
69. Supra no. 35, para no. 2.13.
70. Virendra Dayal, op.cit., p. 45.
71. Section 20 of the Act.
72. Virendra Dayal, op.cit., pp. 45-46.
73. "National Human Rights Institutions : Background and Overview" : Centre for Human Rights, National Human Rights Institutions – Professional Training Series No. 4, United Nations : New York and Geneva, 1995, p. 28.
74. In view of the large number of complaints reaching the NHRC, it has amended the regulations in 1996 to place the complaints before a single-member bench for the quick and efficient handling of the complaints in

normal course. But if single-member bench is of the opinion that the case should be heard by a larger bench, it may refer the case to a larger bench.

75. Virendra Dayal, op. cit., p. 52.
76. Annual Report of the NHRC (1996-97), p. 23.
77. Amnesty Internatinal Report, supra no. 35, pp. 7-8.
78. Supra no.10, p. 18.
79. Section 2 (1) (a) of the Act.
80. Supra no. 35, pp. 14-15.
81. *Ibid.*, p. 5.
82. Annual Report of the NHRC (1999-2000), Annexure No. 12, p. 184.
83. Virendra Dayal, op.cit., p. 46.
84. Section 36 (2) of the Act.
85. Mangari Rajender, op. cit., pp. 57-58.
86. Annual Report of the NHRC (1993-94), para no. 10.1.
87. Mangari Rajender, op. cit. pp. 38-39.
88. Annual Report of the NHRC (1993-94), para no. 10.4.
89. State Human Rights Commissions had been established in Assam, Himachal Pradesh, Jammu and Kashmir, Kerala, Madhya Pradesh, Punjab, Rajasthan, Tamil Nadu and West Bengal, while the states of Bihar, Maharashtra and Orissa has issued notifications constituting the State Human Rights Commissions but they have not yet come into being. Annual Report of the NHRC (1999-2000), paras no. 15.2 – 15.5.
90. Annual Report of the NHRC (1996-97) para no. 8.6.
91. Annual Report of the NHRC (1997-98) para no. 13.3.
92. Annual Report of the NHRC (1994-95) para no. 8.2.
93. Annual Report of the NHRC (1996-97) para no. 8.4.
94. Annual Report of the NHRC (1993-94) para no. 6 to the Annexure No. 6.
95. Annual Report of the NHRC (1997-98) para no. 13.5.
96. "Summary of points raised and findings recorded by the Madras High Court on the setting up of Human Rights Courts", Annual Report of the NHRC (1997-98), Annexure No. VII, pp. 117-120.
97. *Ibid.*
98. Supra no. 35, p.11
99. Annual Report of the NHRC (1995-96) para no. 8.5

100. Ibid, para no. 8.6.
101. Supra no. 35, p. 3.
102. Supra no. 10, para no. 4.4, p. 29.
103. Section 12 (b) of the Act.
104. Section 18 (2) of the Act.
105. Annual Report of the NHRC (1995-96), pp. 64-65.
106. Annual Report of the N HRC (1997-98), para no. 4.2-4.5
107. *Ibid,* para no. Ii, p. 4.
108. Virendra Dayal, op. cit., p. 50.
109. Justice Shivaraj V. Patil, "A Review of the Achievements of the NHRC (1993-2006), *Journal of the NHRC*, Vol. 5, 2006; pp. 153-154.
110. UN Handbook, supra no. 12, p. 11.
111. Section 32 (1) of the Act.
112. Section 32 (2) of the Act.
113. Vijayashri Sirpati, op. cit., p.156.
114. Amnesty International's Report, supra no. 35, p.18.
115. Section 3 (4) of the Act.
116. Section 11(1) (a) of the Act.
117. Section 11(2) and 11(3) of the Act.
118. Annual Report of the NHRC (1993-94), para no. 12.2.
119. *Ibid.*
120. Annual Report of the NHRC (1995-96), para no. 11.4.
121. Section 11(1) (b) of the Act.
122. Arun Kumar Palai, "National Human Rights Commission : Formation, Functioning and Future Prospects", (New Delhi : 1998), pp. 57-58.
123. Annual Report of the NHRC (1993-94), para no. 12.2
124. Annual Report of the NHRC (1994-95), para no. 11.9.
125. Arun Kumar Palai, op. cit., p. 65.
126. Annual Report of the NHRC (1994-95), para no. 11.4.
127. Annual Report of the NHRC (1996-97), paras no. 6.29-6.31.

Chapter IV

Role of the NHRC in the Protection of Human Rights

The implementation of human rights demands both the short-term and long-term approaches. That is why, the functions of the NHRC, as defined under the Act,[1] envisage it a two fold role the protectionist/ interventionist and the promotional / advisory role. The first one follows the short-term approach whereas the second one pursues the long-term approach. Of course, both these approaches are complementary to each other and inter-related as well.[2] This chapter is confined only to the first approach.

The protectionist and interventionist approach is fast-track approach which aims to provide immediate relief to the victims of human rights violations. It also seeks to correct and reform the wrongs and abuses committed against the victims of violations.[3] It may be termed as preventive approach as well. Because, the NHRC is empowered to act '*suo motu* or on a petition presented to it by victim or any person on his behalf, into complaints of violations of human rights or abetment, or negligence in the prevention of such violation, by a public servant.'[4] As the custodian of human rights at the national level, the NHRC is empowered, under the Act, 'to intervene in any proceeding involving allegation of violation of human rights pending before a Court with approval of such court.'[5] As the watch-dog of human rights, the NHRC has power 'to visit under intimation of the State Government, any jail or any other institution under the Central or the State Government, where persons are detained or lodged for purposes of treatment, reformation or protection to study the living conditions of the inmates and make recommendations thereon.'[6]

The above assigned role need not be taken lightly. At the very start, the NHRC was aware of the fact that the credibility of the NHRC depends on its functional autonomy and the transparency of its acts.[7] Its commitment to functional autonomy and transparency of actions becomes evident in its handling of the cases of human rights and evolving an objective approach with regard to various procedures adopted by it.

The establishment of the NHRC was a welcome move. The enthusiastic response of the people is reflected in the fact that in the first six months of its inception, the NHRC received a total of 496 complaints, out of which 274 complaints were rejected and 174 complaints were inquired into. Also 48 matters were finally disposed off with necessary directions.[8] The trust reposed by the people in the NHRC further resulted in the exponential increase in the number of complaints registered with each passing year as shown in the diagram no. 4.1

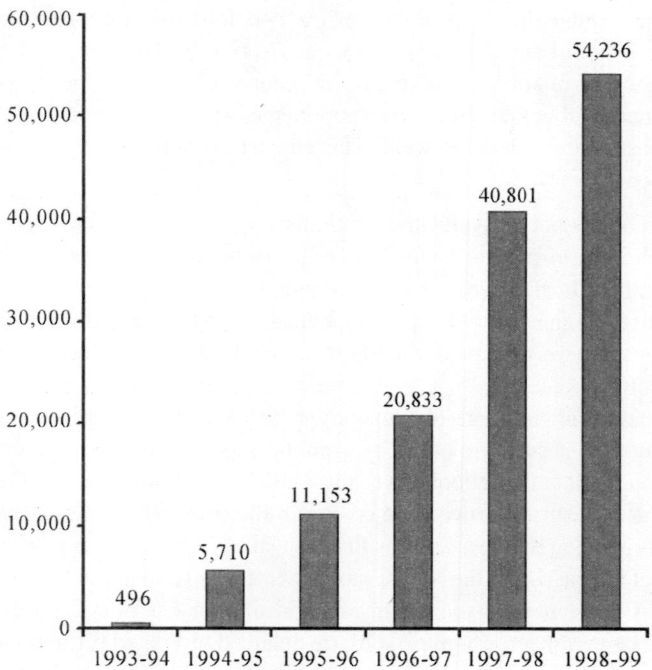

Source : Annual Report of the NHRC

Diagram 4.1: Total Registered Cases – 1993-99.

The increasing work load of the NHRC called for the restructuring and revamping of its administrative setup with a view to improve its efficiency and credibility. The services of the US consultancy giant Mckinsey were hired for this purpose resulting in changes in its working methods. The constitution of single-member benches instead of two-membered bench to deal with complaints helped in disposal of a much larger number of cases at any given point of time. Certain other changes were also made in procedures dealing with the complaints in order to make initial scrutiny more effective. The process of adjusting itself to the demands of fast increasing number of cases would have to be a continuing one and must, in course of time, take the form of higher management technique. The commission also tried to devise new procedures to enable to process certain categories of complaints under its directions at the level below it. Initiatives were taken to identify functionaries who could be entrusted with this responsibility.[9]

The growing number of complaints forced the NHRC to evolve a systematic mechanism to handle them in an efficient manner. This led to the adoption of modern technology by the NHRC. The NHRC is getting cooperation from the National Informatics Centre (NIC) in the computerized working of the NHRC to lend it more efficiency. The NIC has also developed a user-friendly software package to check the status of the complaints.[10] All these efforts are indicative of sincere commitment of the NHRC to attain professional efficiency in the effective protection of human rights.

Priority Areas of the NHRC

No doubt, the NHRC accepts that all human rights are important and they are indivisible; however, looking at the quantum of the case load piled up at the NHRC, it becomes imperative to set the priorities. The NHRC has been prompt in setting it priorities as is evident from its own reports.[11] It has clearly stated its areas of priority that need immediate intervention and relief:

- Civil Liberties (Investigation into the misuse of Terrorist Activities and Disruptive Activities Act).
- Investigate the conduct of army, para-military and police in insurgency affected areas, particularly the cases of fake encounter and extra-judicial killings.
- Rape and murder in police / judicial custody.

- Torture of prisoners and ill-treatment of inmates in remand homes and other places of custody.
- Rights of scheduled castes, scheduled tribes, minorities and women.
- Rights of weaker sections of society such as children specially girl child, child labour, bonded labour and refugees, etc.[12]

The above mentioned areas of priority has been set after considering the fact that the right to life is the mother right of all human rights and therefore, the protection of right to life needs to get the top most priority of the complaints reaching the NHRC fall under this category. Yet the NHRC understands the need to act faster in certain category of complaints involving serious allegations of custodial violence or torture and serious apprehension as to the safety of lives of petitioners. Therefore, the detailed procedural guidelines have been issued to handle such cases as urgent and to put them on the fast-track[13] and the NHRC's response in this regard has been very prompt.

The very first case, taken up by the NHRC after its inception, related to a firing incident in Bij Behera area of Jammu and Kashmir where security forces indulged in indiscriminate firing killing some 60 persons. The NHRC took suo-moto action based on media-reports. After proper investigation and examination of facts, the NHRC recommended the payment of compensation to the victims of firing and also suggested some useful guidelines to the Government of India to review its policy in matter of deployment of security forces with a view to make it human rights friendly.[14] The two fold approach of the NHRC in dealing with cases of human rights abuses, aims at providing the relief to the victims in the form compensation and also prompting the government to reform the system that is insensitive towards human rights.

The cases of disappearances, fake-encounters and extra-judicial killings are abound and represent the gravest form of human rights abuse where again the right to life is at the stake. The NHRC has been regularly receiving complaints about the disappearance of the people and is requested to look into the matter. The diagram no. 4.2 is illustrative of the number of complaints entertained by the NHRC about the disappeared persons. In the year 1994-95, 55 complaints were received, in 1995-96 the number was restricted to 39 while in 1996-97, it shot up to 175 and again dipping down to 12 in the year 1997-98. Finally, in the year 1998-99, the number reached 27. Although, the graph does not explain any particular trend in itself, but it is indicative of the size of the problem.

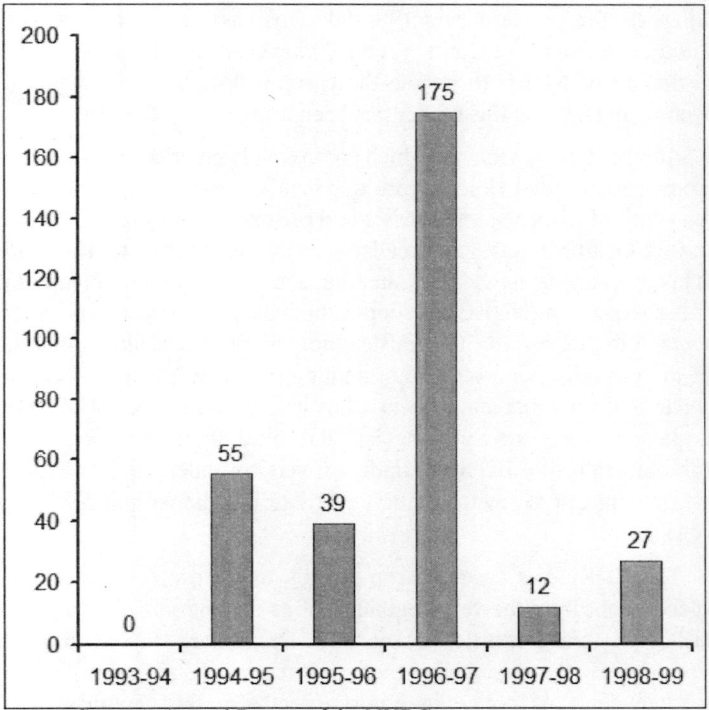

Source : Annual Report of the NHRC

Diagram 4.2: Disappearance – 1993-99.

Closely related with the problem of disappearances is the crime of fake-encounters and extra-judicial killings. The NHRC, acting on the complaint of the Andhra Pradesh Civil Liberties Committee (APCLC) alleging the fake encounters staged by the Andhra Pradesh Police in order to eliminate members of the People's War Group (PWG), their supporters and sympathisers, closely examined the procedure followed in Andhra Pradesh and pronounced that the procedure followed was wrong and the NHRC laid down and indicated the correct procedure to be followed in all such cases. These recommendations have been accepted by the Andhra Pradesh Government.

Custodial Violence

Another important case of extra-judicial killings related to the State of Punjab. It involved alleged mass cremation of victims of indiscriminate killings by the police during 1991-93. This case was entrusted to the NHRC by the Supreme Court. Yet the Union Government questioned the jurisdiction of NHRC to handle the case on time barred ground. The government stand on this matter has been criticised by the media.[16]

Another type of violence which is commonly practiced in our country is known as custodial violence resulting in inhuman treatment, torture and even death of suspects, under-trials and prisoners at various places such as police lock-up, interrogation cells / centres and prisons, etc. The NHRC has taken a serious view of this situation and is deeply committed to stop this barbarism. The NHRC has adopted both the preventive and corrective approach in this regard. Its persistent commitment is evident in the fact that the custodial violence and systemic police and prison reforms are regular subjects of its attention in all of its annual reports.[17] The NHRC has passed severe strictures against the Uttar Pradesh police for the custodial death of a Benaras Hindu University student and ordered the state government to pay the highest ever interim compensation of rupees five lacs.[18]

The NHRC has accorded top priority to the problem of custodial violence right from the very beginning of its coming into existence. The NHRC has issued instructions on 14th December, 1993 to the chief secretaries of all states, asking them to direct all district magistrate and superintendents of police to report directly to the commission any instances of death or rape in police custody within twenty four hours of its occurrence. Failure to send such reports, it was made clear, would lead to a presumption by the commission that an effort was being made to suppress the facts. Subsequent instructions extended the request for such reports to cover deaths in judicial custody as well.[19]

Consequent to the instructions issued by the NHRC regarding the reporting of custodial deaths, the number of reported custodial deaths has increased as shown in the diagram no. 4.3 and 4.4 It is considered a healthy sign as it is a result of more rigorous and better response to the NHRC's instructions that information regarding such tragic occurrences must not be suppressed, but must be reported promptly, and investigated and acted upon there after.[20]

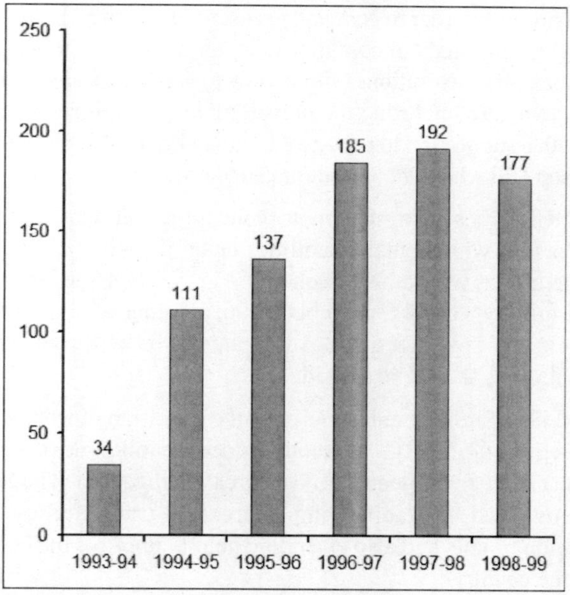

Source : Annual Report of the NHRC

Diagram 4.3: Deaths in Police Custody 1993-99

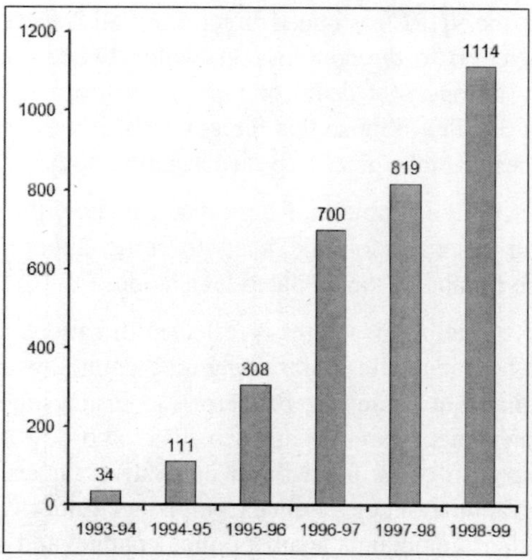

Source : Annual Report of the NHRC

Diagram 4.4: Deaths in Judicial Custody 1993-99

Furthermore, in order to contain the custodial violence the NHRC has also undertaken the study of conditions prevailing in jails, police lockups and other custodial institutions with a view to suggest systemic reforms. It has also gone into analysing the prevailing laws in this regard and has come up with a suggestion to replace the Indian Prison Act of 1894 with a Model Prison Bill which it has undertaken to draft.[21]

The NHRC has also shown its concern about the instances of innocent persons with mental disabilities being illegally held in prisons and being treated as were other prisoners.[22] The NHRC issued instructions to all chief-ministers on 11 September, 1996, pointing out the appropriate provisions in the law in respect of the manner in which persons with mental disabilities should be treated.[23]

The NHRC, further, paid attention to the condition of women held in jai. In this regard, the NHRC has recommended the follow up of the Justice V.R. Krishna Iyer Committee report with greater diligence.[24] The NHRC is actively involved in facilitating increased transparency in the administration of jails and also extending help to improve the conditions of jails in the country.[25]

The NHRC has also dealt with the conditions prevailing in juvenile homes and taken-up the matter on a country wide basis and acted to serve as a catalyst for reform and improvement. Given the reports of violence in such institutions, the NHRC has issued directions to all State Governments asking them to report to the commission, within twenty-four hours of occurrence, any instances of death or rape in such institutions. These instructions run parallel to those that already exist in respect of similar tragic occurrences that take place in police or jail custody.[26]

In dealing with the problem of custodial violence, the NHRC has consistently laid emphasis on the need to bring about institutional reforms and also to modify the outdated legislations.[27]

It's proactive role in this matter is reflected in various promotional initiatives taken by it in the form of training programmes, workshops and seminars etc, aimed at achieving better prison management and also imparting human rights awareness and sensitisation of law enforcement officials.[28] It has also come up with an innovative suggestion for the Police Administration to set up a Police Complaints Authority to reassure the public that their complaints against police conduct and insensitivity would be looked into in all earnest.[29]

Terrorism, Insurgency and Militancy

Terrorism poses a grave threat to enjoyment of human rights. It is both the cause and consequence of human rights violation. Therefore, a delicately balanced approach is needed to tackle the problem arising out of the situation of terrorism, insurgency and militancy. The NHRC has justified the trust of the people in its matured and well-balanced approach asserting its unequivocal commitment to protection of human rights under adverse situation.

While, the NHRC has disapproved the calculated acts of violence perpetrated by terrorists, militants and insurgents[30] and also emphasised the need to fight the menace of terrorism with full state might; it has been very emphatic in pointing out that the rule of law must prevail even in the worst of situation during the course of fight against terrorism and those who breach it must be subjected to the processes of law.[31] Under no circumstances, security-forces be permitted to have a free hand to fight terrorism.

Pursuant to this approach, the NHRC took up a review study of the Terrorist and Disruptive Activities (Prevention) Act, 1987 (TADA) which had been used indiscriminately against innocents in the guise of war against terrorism. The NHRC criticised the law as 'incompatible with our cultural traditions legal history and treaty obligations,' and opposed its renewal.[32] The efforts of the NHRC yielded results when the government decided not to revive the law after its expiry on 23rd May, 1995.[33]

In dealing with the problem arising out of misuse of TADA, despite its expiry, the NHRC continued to work for the freedom of many thousands of under-trails who remained in jails in various states and the union territories under the provision of TADA.[34] It resorted to a three way strategy and worked in collaboration with the state governments and the Supreme Court to facilitate bails in such cases.[35]

Another law dealing with problem of militancy and insurgency also came under the scrutiny of the NHRC. Acting on the representation submitted by an NGO, the NHRC proceeded to examine the Armed Forces (Special Powers) Act, 1958 which extended unlimited powers to the personnels of security forces to carry out searches and to arrest without warrant, to detain and even shoot to kill on grounds of committing or on suspicion of committing certain offences.[36]

Besides reviewing the laws pertaining to handling the situations of terrorism, insurgency and militancy, the NHRC issued guidelines for the security forces and armed forces to observe restraint and to develop respect for human rights.[37] It further urged the security and armed forces to keep the NHRC informed, on the regular basis, of their personnel who, since 1990, have been charged with violation of human rights.[38] This, too has yielded positive results and a decline has been noticed in number of such cases.[39] The NHRC is of the view that the transparency and accountability on the part of the armed forces, as per the recommendation made by the NHRC, will add to the credibility of the armed forces in the conduct of their operations and also discourage unwarranted and propagandist charges against them.[40]

Upholding solidarity with the victims of terrorism, the NHRC has unhesitatingly intervened on their behalf in the states which are, or have been, subject to such violence, recommending enhanced compensation, employment, educational, housing and other facilities as the situation has warranted.[41]

The NHRC also recommended that dialogue between policy makers, the security forces and human rights proponents be sustained, for it could contribute greatly to clarity of thought and action in dealing with insurgency and terrorism.[42] It also supported the political initiatives taken by the government to tackle the problem of terrorism and insurgency.[43]

In its effort to act as an impartial agency to deal with the alleged human rights violation charges against the security forces, particularly in terrorism / insurgency inflicted areas, the NHRC has made repeated recommendations and lobbied for an amendment to Section 19 of the Protection of Human Rights Act, 1993 seeking to bring the army and para-military forces under the closer vigil of the NHRC.[44] But the Union Government's response is negative in this regard.[45] Still, the NHRC continues to persist on its recommendations with a hope that sooner than later, the government will understand the need for the transparency and accountability in ensuring good governance.

Administration of Criminal Justice System

The importance of efficient criminal justice delivery system in the promotion and protection of human rights has not been missed out by the NHRC. In fact, it has been accorded a place of priority on its agenda and finds mention in all of its annual reports regularly.[46] The NHRC is concerned with the state of administration of criminal justice in India and is in the know of its deficiencies both substantive and procedural.[47] Major amongst these include prison population largely consisting of undertrials, the low rate of convictions and proverbial delays in conducting trials.

In this recommendations, the NHRC has emphasised the need to bring about certain institutional changes in the country's legal system to give effect to speedy trials and efficient prosecutorial conduct of trials leading to conviction. In this context, the NHRC has recommended a time-bound programme to embark upon for the speedy clearance of criminal cases in the courts, through the High Courts of the respective states.[48] In terms of changes in the substantive law, it has also recommended a process of progressive and massive decriminalisation of offences now recognised and made culpable as penal offences. Some of other recommendations include introduction of system of plea-bargaining; system of compensation; insulation of police from extraneous pressures; system of Honorary Judicial Magistrates; promoting NGOs for 'Victim Assistance and Service' and for the protection of witnesses in collaboration with police system, and evolution and implementation of appropriate training programmes for members of the magistracy in human rights jurisprudence.[49]

Pursuant to these recommendations of the NHRC and the recommendation of the XI Finance Commission, 1, 734 fast-track courts had been proposed to be set up all over the country to dispose of long pending session cases, important criminal cases and other civil cases during 2000-2005. In many of these courts, retired judicial officers and judicial staff had been engaged. Till 2002, about 1,015 of such additional courts had been set up in the country.[50]

In the matter of revamping the criminal justice system, the government had also set up a committee under the chairmanship of Shri Justice V.S. Malimath with comprehensive terms of reference to suggest measures for efficient criminal justice delivery system.[51]

Rights of Vulnerable Groups

Another priority area of the NHRC relates to the rights of vulnerable groups such as women, children, scheduled castes / scheduled tribes or Dalits, minorities, disabled people and mentally ill people etc. Denial of rights to these social groups is quite rampant and also socially endorsed practice in the country. The NHRC has been particularly engaged to ensure the promotion and protection of rights of these vulnerable groups both by way of *suo motu* action and the basis of complaints.

(A) Women

The question of gender justice is upper most in the mind of NHRC. In order to work in close cooperation with the National Commission for Women, the NHRC has the chairperson of Women's Commission as one of its ex-officio member which provides women's perspective to the NHRC's approach to gender-justice. Considering the varied dimensions of the issue of gender-justice, the NHRC has adopted both the interventionist/preventionist approach as well as correctional and reformist approach. In the cases relating to indignity to women, custodial rapes, dowry-deaths, the NHRC has acted promptly on *suo moto* basis as well as on complaints.

Taking cognizance of a press report about the alleged tattooing of the words *'Jeb Katri'* on the forehead of four women by Amritsar police personnel, the NHRC decided to intervene under Section 12 (b) of the Protection of Human Rights Act, with the due permission of the High Court (where the matter was pending) filing an affidavit through a counsel demanding : (a) investigation be handed over to Central Bureau of Investigation; (b) allow the victims to have their foreheads operated by competent plastic-surgeons of their choice at state cost; and (c) allow interim compensation.[52] The court made a direction accepting all the suggestions of the NHRC.

Another important case related to mass-rape of a woman-social worker named Smt Bhanwari Devi working in rural areas under the State Government's Women Development Programme. The reported acquittal of the accused of rape by the District and Sessions Court in Jaipur and the persisting sense of hostility among the accused persons against the victim made the NHRC to act *suo motu* in the matter seeking a report from the Government of Rajasthan. The intervention of the NHRC compelled the Government of Rajasthan to go into an appeal to the High Court against the judgement of the District and Sessions Court of Jaipur.[53]

Every year, cases of indignity to women have been reported to the NHRC. These cases included crimes of rape, naked parading of women in public, sexual exploitation at the work-place, dowry-deaths, etc. As shown in the diagram no. 4.5, the number of cases reported to the NHRC under this category is much lesser than those reported under the category of police / judicial custodial violence. Yet, the enormity and complexity of the problem related to the gender justice has not waned for the NHRC. Considering the nature of the problem, the NHRC has recommended legal reforms as well as social reforms.

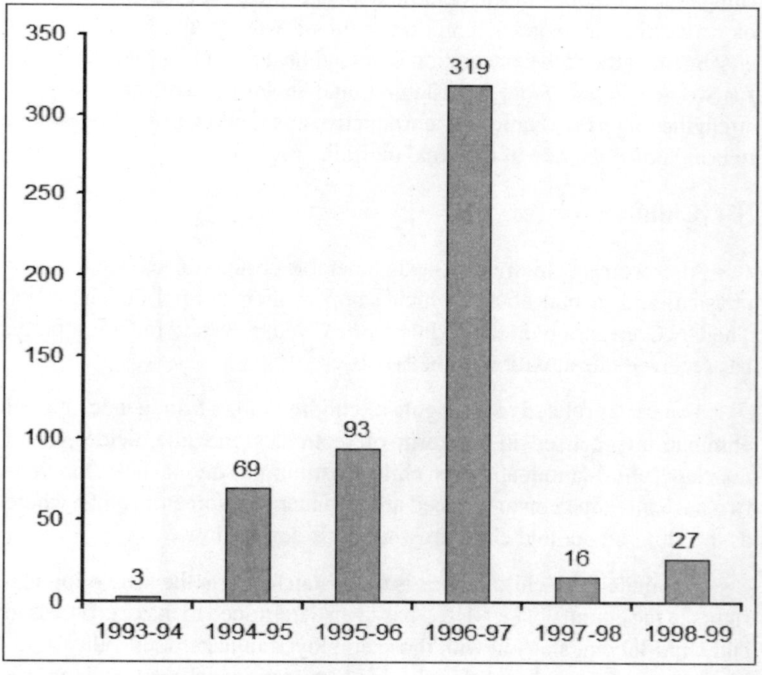

Source : Annual Report of the NHRC

Diagram 4.5: Indignity to Women.

Several laws relating to the status of women, such as the Dowry Prohibition Act, the Sati (Prevention) Act, the Indian Penal Code and the Code of Criminal Procedure, have been reviewed by an Expert Committee set up by the National Commission for Women with whom the NHRC has been interacting regularly. For its part, the NHRC has undertaken the task of making certain recommendations in regard to the amendment of Child Marriage Restraint Act aimed at the menace of child marriages.[54]

The issues of gender-discrimination are also the focus of attention to the NHRC. The implementation of the provisions of the UN Convention on the Elimination of All Forms of Discrimination Against Women, 1986 (CEDAW) to which India has acceded, has been treated as an urgent task.[55] The NHRC has made wide-ranging recommendations in this regard which include the gender sensitisation of health-workers; the training of other key-players in the governance of the country to make them more sensitive to gender-related issues; vigorous and comprehensive national campaign against female-foeticide and female infanticide, *devadasi* system or trafficking in women, empowerment of women through the early enactment of the 85th Constitutional Amendment providing for reservation for women in the State Legislatures and in Parliament; and also the strengthening of the National Reproductive and Child Health Programme to bring down the rate of maternal mortality rate, etc.[56]

(B) Children

After women, children are next vulnerable group subjected to frequent physical and mental abuses which hampers their normal development. The UN Convention on the Rights of the Child, to which India is a party, has received due attention of the NHRC.

The issues related to the rights of children range from gender-biased elimination practised in the form of feoticides and infanticides, child marriage, child-labour and even child prostitution. Among these, the first-two have already been mentioned above under the women's rights, where as the child labour and child prostitution is dealt below.

The malaise of child-labour is a sad statement on the state of human rights in the country. The NHRC has been determined to make progress to end child-labour, starting with those employed in hazardous industries.[57] It recommended quick and effective implementation of the project prepared by the Uttar Pradesh Government for the elimination of child-labour in the glass industry in Firozabad. It further recommended the adoption of appropriate legislation on compulsory primary education, matched with the necessary resources required for this purpose. It also recommended for an early action with regard to amending of the Child Labour (Prohibition and Regulation) Act.[58]

Not satisfied merely by recommending changes in the labour laws, the NHRC waging a war against the child-labour attacked the reprehensible practice of the employment of children as domestic help in the homes of government official's who are expected to know the law better. In this regard, the NHRC recommended to induct an appropriate rule in the Conduct Rules of Government Servants both Central and State inviting a major penalty if found to have employed children as domestic help.[59]

The menacing implication of child prostitution loomed large in the concerns of the NHRC. Considering the destructive nature of the problem on the rights of children, the NHRC has constituted a core-group comprising of the National Commission for Women, the Department of Women and Child Development, selected NGOs and UNICEF to deal with the challenge of rehabilitating children weaned away from prostitution; to press for greater efforts, at the level of SAARC to strengthen laws and to devise cooperative measures to deal with trans-border movements.[60]

The NHRC's concern for the welfare of children is reflected in its taking a serious note of the wide prevalence of iron and iodine deficiency related health problems which cause in large numbers of children in our country being born with mental disabilities. The NHRC has shown its commitment step up the preventive action to remedy the situation.[61]

(C) Scheduled Castes / Tribes or Dalits

Another area of concern for the NHRC is atrocities against the scheduled castes / scheduled tribes or Dalits. They constitute the largest group of people suffering social injustice on a regular basis and are unable to raise voice against it. They are victims of ages old deeply entrenched social biases which get manifested in the practice of untouchability, bonded-labour, torture and inhuman treatment. They are subjected to social and economic discrimination as well as sexual exploitation.

Despite the constitutional and legal abolition of untouchability and human trafficking / bonded-labour, the pernicious practice of untouchability and discrimination against the scheduled castes / tribes or Dalits is still continuing. The NHRC is committed to root out 'untouchability' and prevent atrocities against the scheduled castes / tribes and also to ensure social justice. It has the chairperson of the National Commission of the Scheduled Castes and Scheduled Tribes as one of the ex-officio member of the NHRC to take care of their rights.

The abysmal failure of the government, both the Union and States, to implement the laws prohibiting the practice of manual scavenging, untouchability and bonded labour, has compelled the NHRC to initiate action for effective enforcement of these laws. It took up the matter with various ministries and the chief ministers of all states together with the National Commission for Safai Karamcharies to give impetus to its efforts in evolving suitable measures to eradicate the manual scavenging completely.

It is keeping a close watch on the implementation of laws as well as a national scheme relating to the abolition of this demeaning practice.[62] The NHRC has also recommended for the effective implementation of the provisions of the Protection of Civil Rights Act, 1955 and the Scheduled Castes and Scheduled Tribes (Prevention of Atrocities) Act, 1989.[63]

Similarly, in the matter of bonded-labour system, the NHRC is asked by the Supreme Court to supervise the work relating to the abolition of bonded labour.

The NHRC has initiated action to tackle this problem in a sustained way through a Central Action Group under the leadership of its chairperson and with close cooperation of Special Rapporteur.[64]

The proactive role of the NHRC came to the fore when it intervened to tackle the problem of atrocities on Dalits in Bihar as a result of on-going caste-war between the upper caste landlords and the Dalits. Acting *suo motu,* the NHRC expressed shock at the news of the killing of 21 Dalits in Jahanabad and issued notices to the Chief-Secretary and Director-General of Police, Government of Bihar and directed the state government to grant relief and succour to the members of the families of the deceased and to the injured victims.[65]

The NHRC has also taken note of the problems of denotified and nomadic tribes who constitute almost 2.5 per cent of the population of the country and many of these tribes are treated, for all practical purposes, as habitual offenders and are victims of mob-lynching, arson and police-brutality.

The NHRC formed an Advisory Group in May 1998 to advice it as to the nature of the enquiries it may undertake as well as the recommendations that it can make to deal the issues faced by the denotified and nomadic tribes.[66]

Though, the concern displayed by the NHRC for the rights of the scheduled castes and scheduled tribes or Dalits is quite obvious from the facts stated above, yet this category of complaints does not appear prominently in the annual reports of the NHRC and even the quantum of complaints is much less and is not specifically mentioned in the annual reports as is evident from diagram no. 4.6.

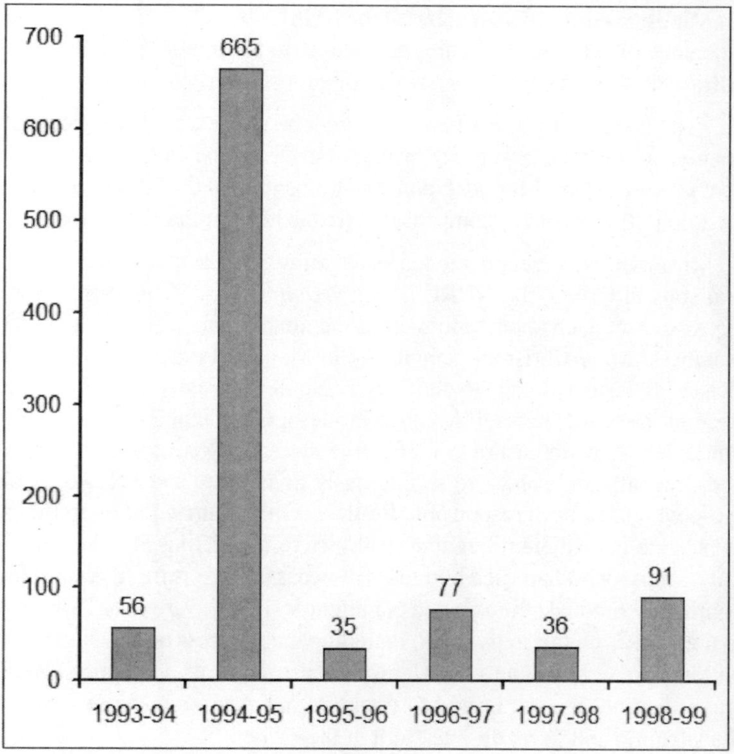

Source : Annual Report of the NHRC

Diagram 4.6: Atrocities on SC/ST – 1993-99.

- 93-94 – Included as 'Others'.
- 94-95 – Included as under the categories : Jail conditions, Bonded. Labour and Others.

Perhaps, the lack of resources necessary to approach the NHRC is one of the reason for the small quantum of complaints by this vulnerable section. Another reason could be that a large number of case of atrocities against them are covered under the category of custodial violence.

(D) Minorities

The protection of the rights of minorities is the constitutional obligation of every government in democracy. Minority rights are included in human rights. Therefore, the Chairperson of the National Commission for Minorities is deemed member of the NHRC. Despite the constitutional guarantee of religious and cultural freedom to the minorities, communal hostility is still quite pervasive, which often results in communal violence.

The NHRC has been approached by one of the kin of the victim of communal riot in Gujarat which broke out in December 1993 following the demolition of Babri Maszid. Upon the intervention of the NHRC, a sum of Rs 2,00,000 was paid as compensation to the heirs of the riot-victim.[67]

In another case relating to the killing of Australian missionary and his two sons in Orissa, the NHRC acting *suo motu* on 25th January, 1999, expressed its deep shock and pain at the attacks carried out against the members of the Christian community in Madhya Pradesh, Gujarat and Orissa. It issued notice to the Union Home Secretary and the Chief Secretaries of the States of Madhya Pradesh, Gujarat and Orissa, to take immediate steps to ensure that effective measures were taken to control and prevent such events, to scrupulously investigate and bring to book those who have been responsible for the events occurring in these states, to provide immediate relief and assistance to the victims and the next of kin of those who had died and take all necessary measure to restore the confidence amongst the affected communities. They were asked to report to the NHRC on the steps taken, including the progress of investigations, within two weeks. The NHRC further instructed its Director-General (Investigation) to visit Orissa forthwith to make an on the spot study of the situation and to report back to it at the earliest.[68]

The NHRC has also drawn the attention of leaders of all sections of society towards growing pattern of violence and intolerance which is threatening the culture of human rights. In its endeavour to promote human rights culture, the NHRC indicated its intention to revive its own investigation into certain complaints relating to communal violence that took place in Bombay in January 1993 and expressed its dismay on the decision of the Government of Maharashtra to terminate the Srikrishna Commission which was investigating the Bombay communal riots of 1993. It asked for the restoration of the Srikrishna Commission[69], which got revived after all.[70]

(E) Rights of Disabled Persons

The rights of disabled persons have always been on the agenda of the NHRC. It has recommended the early enactment of an appropriate law on behalf of such persons whose rights must be respected and supported.

In 1995, the Persons with Disability (Equal Opportunities, Protection of Rights and Full Participation) Act was enacted. The NHRC pressed for the adoption of this Act and called for the framing of rules and regulations concerning the effective implementation of this law. It also urged to expedite the matter which led to the Ministry of Welfare issuing a notification promulgating the rules required under the Act. The NHRC further recommended to speed up the process of the appointments and other practical measures. The NHRC has also been interacting with state governments to take-stock of the facilities provided to persons with disabilities, so that it can use this information in assessing the compliance of the Act and also in examining the specific complaints that it receives.[71]

The NHRC continued to receive complaints as well as suggestions regarding assistance to persons with disabilities. The Handicapped Welfare Federation, Delhi raised the issue of the right to postal ballot for the disabled persons. After examining the matter, the NHRC has referred to the matter to the Election Commission.[72]

(F) Rights of the Mentally Ill Persons

Of late, the rights of mentally ill have drawn the attention of human rights propagators including the United Nations. Even the Indian Constitution recognises the right to equal status to this vulnerable group. The human rights perspective insists upon the rights of mentally ill person even in hospital which includes the right to bodily integrity, to privacy, to appropriate treatment, to be protected from cruelty and involuntary servitude and a right to community and family life once improved rather than a life of incarceration. The Mental Health Act, 1987 is aimed at incorporating therapeutic and rehabilitatory approach towards mentally ill.

Despite the existence of the Mental Health Act, 1987 and the Supreme Court directive on the minimum facilities to be available in mental hospital, the conditions in mental hospitals are pathetic. The NHRC has taken an initiative in this matter and has entrusted a research project on 'Quality Assurance of Mental Hospitals' to the National Institute of Mental Health and Neuro-Sciences (NIMHANS), Bangalore, with a view to seek professional expertise to make recommendations having a positive bearing on the human rights of those suffering mental disabilities.[73]

Apart from its own initiative, the Supreme Court has asked the NHRC to be involved in the supervision of the functioning of the Agra, Gwalior and Ranchi mental hospitals.[74]

Right to Freedom of Press, Expression and Association

The issues relating to right to freedom of speech, expression and association have also drawn the attention of the NHRC. On a complaint filed by the Andhra Pradesh Union of Working Journalists, in which intimidation of journalists by the police and targetting of their Union by the police was reported, the NHRC took strong exception to the conduct of policemen involved and recommended their prosecution. Similarly, another complaint was received from the Writers in Prison Committee about the disappearance of an employee of *Ajeet,* a daily newspaper from Punjab. The NHRC directed the Punjab Government to take up a time-bound investigation in the matter and report back to the NHRC.[75]

In the case of reported ban on the distribution of Salman Rushdie's latest book titled, *Moore's Last Sigh* by the Customs Collectorate, the NHRC swung into action *suo motu* seeking an explanation from the Home Ministry and the Central Board of Excise and Customs. In response to that the Home Ministry informed the NHRC that the matter did not fall within the Protection of Human Rights Act, yet considering the probable impact of the action, the government has decided to permit the distribution of the said book. The NHRC's view as to its competence under the Act differed from the government, however, it welcomed its decision to lift the ban.[76]

The NHRC has also been approached by a number of NGOs and academic institutions from India and abroad to intervene for the restoration of their right to association as the Government of Andhra Pradesh had issued a circular preventing teachers and other faculty members of universities from associating themselves with the Andhra Pradesh Civil Liberties Committee (APCLC). In response to the NHRC's notice, the Government of Andhra Pradesh decided not to take further action in this matter.[77]

Other Category of Rights

Acting on the premise that human rights whether civil and political, economic, social and cultural are, as in the words of Vienna Declaration and Programme of Action, 1993 universal, indivisible, interdependent and inter-related, the NHRC has taken up the cases relating to right to food, right to health, right to education, right to development, etc.

Right to Food

Taking cognizance of the matter relating to alleged starvation deaths in some parts of Orissa, the NHRC deputed a Special Rapporteur to look into the whole issue and submit his observations on the prevailing state of affairs.

The NHRC besides reviewing the implementation of various relief measures, also issued several directives to the administration to hasten the pace of relief measures in the affected areas. It also emphasised the need to implement a better public distribution system, facilitate drinking water and provide basic health care together with the need to speed up programmes relating to land reforms, afforestation, soil-conversation and literacy as long-term measures to improve the quality of life. The NHRC continued to monitor the matter.[78]

Right to Health

Recognising the fact that Right to Health is integral to right to life, the NHRC has taken cognizance of various complaints relating to supply of fluoride or arsenic poisoned drinking water, the problem of iron and iodine defficient diet of young expectant mothers and industrial health hazards, etc.

The NHRC took a serious note of the wide prevalence of iron and iodine deficiency related health problems which result in large numbers of children in our country being born with mental disabilities. It also puts expectant mothers to the risks of anaemia leading to loss of life during child birth. The NHRC has exhorted the concerned ministries and departments to take remedial measures necessary for the prevention of congenital mental disabilities.[79]

Similarly, the NHRC has also responded positively to complaints that drinking water supplies in vast stretches of Andhra Pradesh and West Bengal are poisoned by flouride and arsenic causing slow-death to innumerable people living in these areas.[80]

Another grave threat posed to the health of both the workers and common people is caused due to industrial hazards. The NHRC has also taken up the matter relating to the rights of victims in cases of industrial hazard. The NHRC made recommendations regarding the payment of adequate compensation to the victims of industrial hazard and also advised the state government to do the insurance of workers employed in hazardous industries.[81]

The NHRC has also acted sternly in the reported case of deaths of children caused by malnutrition and water-borne diseases together with the lack of adequate medical facilities. The NHRC found the negligence of the state health machinery responsible for this tragic incident and made recommendations for compensation and the improvement of health services.[82]

Right to Education

Right from its inception, the NHRC made a very strong plea to make the right to education a fundamental right under the constitution, emphasising the close linkage between the right to education and the enjoyment of human rights. The right to education, if fulfilled, would itself be the strongest weapon in the fight against the abuse of human rights in general and particularly to fight the menace of child-labour and other forms of child abuses.[83]

Right to Development

Though right to development has been recognised as a human right, however, the complex nature of this right has caused several humanitarian problems which have drawn the attention of the NHRC. These problems relate to the issues pertaining to internally displaced people and their rehabilitation, rights of indigenous population and right to clean and healthy environment.

In August 1996, the NHRC intervened on the complaint from the National Alliance of People's Movement to take the rights of the persons marginalised by the construction of Bagri Dam in Madhya Praesh.[84] The NHRC continued to receive complaints from different areas of the country alleging inadequacies or indifference in the rehabilitation of communities, more particularly members of disadvantaged groups, when they have been displaced or otherwise adversely affected by mega projects.[85]

After examining all the cases individually, the NHRC thought of appointing a special rapporteur to make extensive study of rehabilitation policies of the governments and make suggestions for a common national policy in this regard.[86]

In another instance, the NHRC received a complaint alleging that the Van Gujjars living in the forest area falling under the proposed Rajaji National Park, Dehradun were being harassed and tortured by the staff of the park and not allowed to fetch fodder for their animals, sell milk or have access to medical aid as an ambulance was not being allowed into the area causing loss of human life. The NHRC directed a special rapporteur to examine the whole matter and made efforts to find a satisfactory solution of this human problem.[87]

Rights of AIDS Victims

The issue of the rights of AIDS victims was brought to the attention of the NHRC by an NGO from Andhra Pradesh. It complained about the forcible HIV testing of nearly 500 sex-workers of Mumbai by the police without providing them any counselling.

The NHRC gave a serious thought to this grave question considering the complex and far-reaching implications of the whole issue. It received the technical and expert assistance from UNAIDS while evolving its recommendations. Before making any kind of recommendations on this issue, the NHRC did not hesitate to educate itself on such a technical issue.[88]

Rights of the Aged Persons

A plea to the NHRC was made to take up voluntarily the cases relating to abuse of rights of elderly persons by the Help Age India.[89] Responding to this plea, the NHRC team held discussions with the area police to help rehabilitate an eighty year old woman who was without any shelter.[90]

Rights of the Cyclone Affected People

Taking *suo motu* cognizance of the situation caused by the Super Cyclone in the coastal districts of Orissa in October 1999, the NHRC established immediate contact with its special representative in Bhubaneshwar, asked its team to visit the area, interact with the officials at different levels and report back, so as to enable it to decide how best to be of assistance to the state government in the relief and rehabilitation effort. It made specific recommendations in respect of the relief, reconstruction and rehabilitation work. It also undertook to monitor the compliance of its recommendations made to the state government.[91]

Economic Rights

The NHRC has been approached with several complaints relating to the denial of economic rights to the plantation workers, landless labourers and tribals. It took *suo motu* cognizance of a media report highlighting the attack on the procession taken out in support of the labour struggle of plantation workers in Tirunelveli, in which 17 persons lost their life. The NHRC issued a notice to the state government in this regard. In response to the notice, the state government instituted a Commission of Inquiry and made a payment of Rupees two lacs to each of the families of the dead. Similarly, in another case of exploitation of tribals by landlords / mafia in Uttar Pradesh, the NHRC directed the state government to observe the necessary recommendations made by it.[92]

The NHRC has also focussed its attention to the problems of tribals living in poor economic conditions, held in bondage and forced to work in slave-like conditions, wages paid to them far below the minimum fixed by the government. Looking to the gravity of the situation, the NHRC constituted an expert-committee to undertake the study of the whole matter and to suggest proper course of action. The matter was closely monitored by the NHRC.[93]

One more type of economic exploitation based on gender-discrimination was brought to the notice of the NHRC. It related to the disparities in maternity leave of the employees of private schools in West Bengal.[94] The NHRC, in fulfillment of Article 11 of CEDAW (UN Convention on the Elimination of Discrimination Against Women), directed the West Bengal Government to undertake a review of the existing rules / codes and to bring about uniformity by ensuring appropriate provision for the grant of 120 days maternity leave to teaching and non-teaching employees in the schools of that state.[95]

Rights of the Refugees

The plight of Chakma refugees in Arunachal Pradesh was brought to the notice of the NHRC which took up the matter with the state government in 1994. Further again, the NHRC received complaints alleging serious 'State-supported' violations of human rights, particularly the serving of quit notices on the refugees, the NHRC after issuing directions to the state government twice in 1995, moved a petition in the Supreme Court under Article 21 of the Constitution seeking direction for Arunachal

Pradesh Government to enforce the right to life of 6,500 Chakma / Hajong refugees.[96]

In another case, the NHRC took cognizance of the complaint relating to non-supply of relief material to Kuki refugees in Manipur. In response to the notice by the NHRC, the state government made special efforts to redress the suffering of Kuki refugees.[97]

Taking a broader view of the problems relating to the refugees, the NHRC emphasised on the need for India to develop a national policy and possibly a national law, fully in consonance with the 1951 United Nations Convention relating to the status of refugees and the 1967 Protocol on the subject recounted its earlier reports. It also persuaded the Government of India to look into the possibility of signing the Convention on the Status of Refugees and the 1967 Protocol on this subject.[98]

Reviewing the Existing International and National Legislation

In order to prevent the abuse of human rights, the NHRC has been empowered to study, examine and formulate reforms in the existing laws under the sub-sections (d) and (f) of the Section 12 of the Act.[99] It is quite a challenging job which the NHRC has taken earnestly right from the time of its inception.

The most controversial legislation reviewed by the NHRC was the Terrorist and Disruptive Activities (Prevention) Act, 1987 which was dropped as a result of the great job done by the NHRC in this regard.[100] Another important law reviewed was the Armed Forces (Special Powers) Act, 1958. Relating to this Act, the NHRC extended all help to the Supreme Court in framing necessary guidelines with a view to eliminate the anti-human rights ethos from it.[101]

The NHRC also undertook a thorough examination of Narcotic Drugs and Psychotropic Substance (NDPS) Act, 1985 to find out the cause of prolonged and unreasonable detention as alleged in numerous complaints to it. It discovered that there was an inadequacy of courts to deal with NDPS cases. It approached the concerned ministry with proposals to make desired amendments to the existing law and remove the obstacle in the speedy dispensation of justice.[102]

The NHRC has examined the whole lot of legislations relating to the status of women and sought the expert advice on the subject and then has made concrete suggestions for the necessary amendments to the existing laws and for the enactment of new laws. Similarly, in the cases of child-rights and the disabled persons rights, the NHRC has come up with positive ideas for the effective implementation of these rights.

The concerns of the NHRC are not restricted to its national obligations alone. It is equally concerned about India's international obligation under various human rights instruments to which it is a party. It keeps on reminding the Government of India of its obligation to submit timely periodic status-reports under various treaty laws. It is always ready to offer its assistance in the preparation of these reports. It also monitors the country status-reports submitted by India as well as the comments of the concerned treaty-bodies.[103]

To sum up the discussion, the role of the NHRC in the protection of human rights has several dimensions. It involves interventionist role where it comes to the rescue of victims of human rights abuses as it did in the case of Chakma refugees.[104] The interventionist role may be played by taking *suo motu* action as well. Another important role played by the NHRC is monitoring role which is very significant from the point of view of effective implementation of human rights.[105] In this role, the NHRC acts as the watch-dog of human rights. Other dimensions of its role include advisory and recommendatory role which are of immense value in guiding the policy-makers. Another significant role played by the NHRC is in its rendering assistance to the Supreme Court whenever it is asked to do so.[106] The NHRC has also played a proactive role in the protection of human rights, encouraging the efforts of the government in ensuring the observance of human rights.[107] Finally, the NHRC's role has been characterised by result-oriented and innovative approaches in dealing with the protection of human rights. To conclude, the NHRC has evolved different strategies to meet the challenge of protection of human rights.

References

1. Section 12, The Protection of Human RightsAct, 1993.
2. Annual Report of the NHRC, (1994-95) para 2.3.
3. *Ibid.*, para 2.2.
4. Section 12 (a), The Protection of Human Rights Act, 1993.
5. *Ibid.*, Section 12 (b).
6. *Ibid.*, Section 12 (c).
7. Annual Report of the NHRC (1993-1994), para 4.1.
8. *Ibid.*, para 5.1.

9. Annual Report of the NHRC (1996-97), para 9.4, See 'NHRC Starts Administrative Revamp move...' *The Asian Age* (New Delhi), 24 Oct, 1997.
10. Annual Report of the NHRC (1994-95), paras 11.5 and 11.7.
11. Annual Report of the NHRC (1993-94), para 4.4.
12. Annual Report of the NHRC (1994-95), para 3.1-3.6.
13. Annual Report of the NHRC (1997-98), Annexure No. 1, Practice Direction No. 8 dated 23rd February, 1998.
14. Annual Report of the NHRC (1993-94), pp. 11-12.
15. Annual Report of the NHRC (1996-97), Annexure No. VI, pp. 103-105.
16. G.S. Bhargava, "Focus on Civil Liberty", *Hindustan Times* (New Delhi), 9th December, 1997.
17. See Annual Reports of the NHRC (1993-99), Custodial Violence and Systemic Police and Prison Reforms constitute an essential component of all annual reports of the NHRC.
18. Annual Report of the NHRC (1997-98), p. 60.
19. See Annexure No. IV, Annual Report of the NHRC (1993-94) and also Annual Report of the NHRC (1997-98), para 3.7.
20. Annual Report of the NHRC (1997-98), para 3.8.
21. Annual Report of the NHRC (1996-97), paras 3.47-3.48.
22. *Ibid.*, para 3.49.
23. *Ibid.*,
24. *Ibid.*, para 3.50.
25. *Ibid.*, paras 3.52-3.55.
26. *Ibid.*, paras 3.58-3.59.
27. See Annual Reports since 1993-94. The NHRC has recapitulated and reiterated certain recommendations of th Indian Law Commission (with regard to the Indian Evidence Act, 1872 and the Code of Criminal Procedure) and also the National Police Commission.
28. Annual Report of the NHRC (1996-97), pp. 47-51; Annual Report of the NHRC (1997-98), p.37 and Annual Report of the NHRC (1998-99) p. 47.
29. Annual Report of the NHRC (1998-99), para 3.31; Also, Kapoor, H.L. "Human Rights in the face of police excesses" in *National Herald* (New Delhi), April 26, 1995.
30. Annual Report of the NHRC (1996-97), para 3.4.

31. *Ibid.*, para 3.8.
32. *Ibid.*
33. Annual Report of the NHRC (1995-96), para 4.1.
34. Till 13th June, 1995, 6060 such cases were reported.
35. Annual Report of the NHRC (1995-96), para 4.2.
36. *Ibid.*, para 4.3.
37. Annual Report of the NHRC (1993-94), Annexure No. V, pp. 47-49.
38. Annual Report of the NHRC (1996-97), para 3.14.
39. *Ibid.*
40. Annual Report of the NHRC (1997-98), para 3.2.
41. *Ibid.*, para 3.18.
42. Annual Report of the NHRC (1996-97), paras 3.10-3.11.
43. *Ibid.*, Summary of the Report and Principal Recommendations, para 6.
44. Supra No. 40.
45. Memorandum of Action Taken Report, Ministry of Home Affairs, Government of India, December 2000, para XIX.
46. Annual Report of the NHRC (1994-95), para 3.3, p.7.
47. Annual Report of the NHRC (1998-99), paras 3.37-3.40.
48. *Ibid.*, para 3.41.
49. See Annual Reports of the NHRC (1996-97), pp. 30-31, (1997-98), p. 20 and (1998-99), p. 20-22.
50. Memorandum of Action Taken Report, Ministry of Home Affairs, Government of India, December 2000, p. 27.
51. *Ibid.*, p. 28.
52. Annual Report of the NHRC (1993-94), pp. 23-24.
53. Annual Report of the NHRC (1995-96), pp. 56-57.
54. Annual Report of the NHRC (1994-95), para 5.9.
55. Annual Report of the NHRC (1993-94), para 7.5.
56. Annual Report of the NHRC (1999-2000), para 2.21.
57. Annual Report of the NHRC (1993-94), para 5.7.
58. Ibid, Annexure VII, paras 10-11.
59. Annual Report of the NHRC (1996-97), paras 5.8-5.9.
60. *Ibid.*, paras 5.14-5.18.

61. *Ibid.*, paras 5.12-5.13.
62. Annual Report of the NHRC (1998-99), paras 11.1-11.6.
63. Annual Report of the NHRC (1999-2000), para 2.39.
64. Annual Report of the NHRC (1998-99), paras 9.1-9.6.
65. *Ibid.*, case no. 3116/4/98-99, p. 97.
66. *Ibid.*, paras 12.1-12.3.
67. Annual Report of the NHRC (1995-96), pp. 70-71.
68. Annual Report of the NHRC (1998-99), pp. 94-97.
69. Annual Report of the NHRC (1995-96), paras, 3.41-3.42.
70. Memorandum of Action Taken Report on annual report of the NHRC (1995-96), Ministry of Home Affairs, Govenrment of India, para XVIII.
71. Refer to Annual Reports of the NHRC for the years 1993-94, 1994-95, 1995-96, 1996-97 and 1997-98.
72. Annual Report of the NHRC (1997-98), para 6.3.
73. *Ibid.*, paras 7.1-7.6.
74. *Ibid.*, paras 8.1-8.11.
75. Annual Report of the NHRC (1995-96), para 3.43.
76. *Ibid.*, para 3.44.
77. Annual Report of the NHRC (1997-98), p. 63.
78. Annual Report of the NHRC (1998-99), p. 91.
79. Annual Report of the NHRC (1996-97), para 5.12.
80. *Ibid.*, para 2.15. Also, see Annual Report of the NHRC (1994-95), pp. 37-39.
81. See Annual Report of the NHRC (1995-96), pp. 66-67; Annual Report of the NHRC (1998-99), pp. 88-89; and Annual Report of the NHRC (1999-2000), p. 126-127.
82. Annual Report of the NHRC (1994-95), pp. 37-39.
83. See Annual Reports of the NHRC right from 1994-95 onwards on the issue of children rights.
84. Annual Report of the NHRC (1996-97), para 5.22-5.24.
85. Annual Report of the NHRC (1998-99), para 6.3.
86. Annual Report of the NHRC (1998-99), para 6.4 and Annual Report of the NHRC (1999-2000), paras 6.1-6.3.
87. Case No. 14971/24/97-98, Annual Report of the NHRC (1998-99), pp. 89-90.

88. Annual Report of the NHRC (1997-98), p. 33.
89. *Times of India* (New Delhi), 19 March, 1998.
90. *Times of India* (New Delhi), 22 March, 1998.
91. Annual Report of the NHRC (1999-2000), paras 6.4-6.10.
92. *Ibid.*, paras 6.11-6.14.
93. *Ibid.*, para 6.15.
94. Case No. 16295/96-97, Annual Report of the NHRC (1998-99), p. 85
95. Annual Report of the NHRC (1998-99), pp. 86-87.
96. Annual Report of the NHRC (1995-96), pp. 64-65.
97. *Ibid.*, pp. 65-66.
98. Annual Report of the NHRC (1999-2000), pp. 45-46.
99. The Protection of Human Rights Act, 1993.
100. Annual Report of the NHRC (1995-96), para 4.1.
101. Annual Report of the NHRC (1997-98), paras 4.1-4.5.
102. Annual Report of the NHRC (1995-96), para 4.4.
103. Annual Report of the NHRC (1998-99). para 4.13 and Annual Report of the NHRC (1999-2000), para 4.10.
104. Supra no. 96.
105. Supra no. 103.
106. Annual Report of the NHRC (1996-97, para 4.4.
107. *Ibid.*, para 3.11.

Chapter V

Role of the NHRC in the Promotion of Human Rights

The promotion of respect and realisation of human rights cannot be ensured by relying on external means alone which are discussed in the preceding chapter. It can be brought about by addressing the root causes of the malady which is internal and requires attitudinal and cultural changes. That's why, the NHRC has been entrusted with the responsibility to play active role in the promotion of human rights culture in the country.

The promotional role of the NHRC is well spelt out in the Protection of Human Rights Act, 1993. As per the Act, the promotional functions of the NHRC include : (a) to study treaties and other international instruments on human rights and make recommendations for their effective implementation; (b) to undertake and promote research in the field of human rights; (c) to spread human rights literacy among various sections of society and promote awareness of the safeguards available for the protection of these rights through publications, the media, seminars and other available means; (d) to encourage the efforts of non-governmental organisation and institutions working in the field of human rights; and (e) such other functions as it may consider necessary for the promotion of humans rights.[1]

The cultivation of human rights culture requires a long term approach for the promotion of human rights awareness. The NHRC, right from its inception, gave it a top priority and worked out a systematic strategy to spread human rights literacy among the masses and also the governing elite. Towards this end, it resorted to the mobilisation of education system at all levels, holding training programmes for administrators, security personnels, professionals and others. Methods such as seminars, conferences, publications, research-studies, publicity-campaigns and other media methods were adopted to create public awareness by all possible means. With a view to keep India in the vanguard of the world-wide movement to promote and protect human rights, the NHRC has interacted with external groups and organisations on a regular basis. It has also promoted the role of the non-governmental organisations in the protection and promotion of human rights.

Human Rights Literacy and Awareness

Recognising the significance of human rights literacy both in terms of present and future perspectives, the NHRC identified three key-sectors of our democratic polity for the purpose of imparting human rights education. These sectors included educationists, the executive authority at all levels and political parties.[2]

As a first step towards mobilising education system, the NHRC made a request to all political parties to constitute Human Rights Cells at the Central, State and District levels of their organisation specifically charged with the responsibility of promoting and protecting human rights. It also requested them to remain in continuing touch with the NHRC in this regard. These cells were expected to serve a dual purpose to propagate and thus promote a climate conducive to human rights.[3] Similarly, the state governments were also approached to initiate moves to impart appropriate training in human rights with a view to sensitise the administration to show respect to human rights. Lastly and most importantly, the National Council of Educational Research and Training (NCERT) and the University Grants Commission (UGC) were also approached to introduce human rights education as an essential component at all levels of education.[4]

Mobilisation of Educational System

The promotion of human rights literacy is a task that calls for great perseverance, deep and lasting commitment, not only on the part of the NHRC, but also on the part the state. That is why, the NHRC sought to mobilise the educational system at all levels to impart human rights education nation-wide. It approached the Ministry of Human Resource Development and the Department of Education to initiate the steps for the purpose of including human rights education as an essential component of national educational curriculum.[5]

The prime educational bodies such as the University Grants Commission (UGC), the National Council of Educational Research and Training (NCERT) and the National Council for Teacher-Education (NCTE) have been roped in to prepare materials for the education at various levels of schooling. The NCERT has prepared a source book on Human Rights as a guide for teachers and others, a project in which the NHRC fully collaborated, making specific suggestions as to its contents. The NCERT was also asked to undertake a review of existing text books with a view to eliminate from them those passages that were inimical to human rights or that distorted them. Steps have been initiated to encourage the inclusion of alternative material sensitive to human rights.[6] On the recommendation on the NHRC, the *Source Book on Human Rights* was translated into Hindi and other regional languages for wider use.[7]

As a next step to imparting human rights education at the school level, modules for teacher-training relevant to teaching at various levels were prepared. For this purpose, a national level training programme on 'Human Rights and National Values for Teacher Educators' was organised by the National Council for Teacher Education (NCTE).[8] In addition, two video films have been made of the modules and a Hindi version of these modules have also been developed.[9] For the propagation of human rights literacy, these modules were adopted by the distant education institution named the National Open School as well.[10]

At the higher education level, the NHRC approached the universities with the proposal to induct the subject of human rights in their curriculum, undertake research and publication and conduct seminars on human rights. It also suggested the linkage between the academic community and the non-governmental organisations.[11] Consequent to the NHRC's suggestion, the University Grants Commission appointed a Standing Committee on human rights education at the university level to bring out a degree of uniformity in the standard of teaching of human rights in different universities.[12]

In a major effort to establish a center of excellence for human rights education, the NHRC has set-up an 'Institute for Human Rights Education, Research and Documentation' at the National Law School of India University (NLSIU), Bangalore.[13] In addition, it has endowed a chair for rupees thirty lacs in the National Law School of India University for the said institute.[14]

The NHRC is of the view that human rights education does not end with the academic institutions. It believes that all elements of civil society need to be brought into the fold : the bench and the bar, administrators and defence personnel, doctors and scholars, politicians and trade unionists, public and private sector employees and members of the fourth estate, to mention a few.[15]

Agreeing with the NHRC, the Union Government set up a National Committee consisting of representatives from various ministries and departments to formulate a National Action Plan for human rights education and to coordinate its implementation.[16]

Apart from mobilisation of education system for the purpose of incorporation of human rights education, the NHRC has also made use of informal educational methods for spreading human rights literacy. With the declaration of the UN Decade for Human Rights Education (1995-2005), it played a catalytic role in the drawing up of a National Action Plan for observing the UN Decade as well as to commemorate the 50th Anniversary of the Universal Declaration of Human Rights (UDHR) during 1997-1998.[17]

Human Rights Education for Police Personnel

Recognising the fact that the largest number of human rights violations are result of insensitive and ignorant police force's high-handedness, the NHRC has given top priority to revamp the training and re-training of police personnel so as to make them more aware of, and sensitive to human rights considerations.

As a consequence to the NHRC's initiatives, the Sardar Vallabhbhai Patel National Police Academy in Hyderabad introduced the teaching of human rights in its courses and also included sensitisation programmes as an essential component of its training courses. The NHRC has extended all possible help in this endeavour. It is convinced that training programmes, when properly structured and conducted, can have a most valuable effect on police personnel and improve their responses even in provocative situations.[18]

The NHRC has also devised a three-tier syllabus for various ranks of the police service, ranging from constables to senior officers. This module has proved useful in the training of all cadres of police force at the state level and training materials are increasingly being prepared in the regional languages for their wide application.[19]

The NHRC is always receptive to the innovations in police practice and encourages the participation of members of its own Investigation Division in courses being conducted both at home and abroad.[20]

Human Rights Education for Para-military and Armed Forces Personnel

The importance of human rights education for the personnel of Para-military and armed forces has not been lost on the NHRC, specially in the light of the fact of their fighting against insurgencies and terrorism. Moreover, the limited mandate given to the NHRC under the statute in the matter of paramilitary and armed forces, makes it imperative on the part of the NHRC to persuade them to educate and sensitise their personnel to human rights considerations. The NHRC has contacted the higher functionaries of these organisations for the purpose of impressing upon them the need for the cultivation of human rights culture in their respective forces.[21]

Encouraged by the positive response from the leadership of the para-military and armed forces, the NHRC has advised them on continued basis on a variety of matters, including those relating to the training of the personnel at all levels. The functionaries of the NHRC paid regular visits to their academies and headquarters to give talks on human rights and answer their queries and remove their doubts. The International Committee of the Red Cross (ICRC) has also been involved to enlighten them on humanitarian jurisprudence. Methods such as debate and discussions have been adopted to make the whole exercise interesting and participatory instead of lecturing.[22]

The NHRC has made sustained efforts to ensure that the para-military forces continued to improve the quality of their training in human rights matter. Towards this end, a core-group was set up to prepare a common training syllabus for the paramilitary forces with the approval of the NHRC. Six out of the seven central police organisations have adopted this syllabus in their training curriculum.[23]

Human Rights Education for Political Parties

In a democratic polity like ours, the political parties, role in creating a human-rights conducive culture is quite significant. Considering this fact, the NHRC approached the top-leadership of various political parties and top functionaries of Parliament and state legislatures to seek their support and suggestions for the promotion of human rights culture in the country.[24]

Besides suggesting the constitution of human rights cells at all levels of the party organisation, the NHRC made a request to the party leaders to oversee the conduct of their members. Each party was also requested to designate a senior leader to liase with the NHRC in regard to human rights matters. The NHRC also made specific recommendations as to the manner in which they could monitor the conduct of their cadres.[25]

In a parliamentary democracy, political parties are important constituent of decision-making process. That's why, the NHRC intensified its efforts to impress upon the political parties the need to include the issue of free and compulsory elementary education for the children of India in their party manifestoes for the impending General Elections.[26] Thus, the NHRC has tried to play the role of an interest group for the purpose of promotion of human rights by lobbying political parties to work for the realisation of human rights.[27]

The NHRC does not hesitate to reproach the political parties whenever they indulge in irresponsible behaviour. It has recommended that political parties should have a clear code of conduct to govern the behaviour of their cadres in matters affecting human rights of the people of this country and the transgressions of such a code be dealt with severely. It has also advised greater restraint and moderation by political parties in dealing with issues sensitive to human rights.[28]

Seminars and Workshops

The NHRC has made use of seminars and workshops extensively for the purpose of spreading human rights education in the country. These informal methods of teaching are very effective ways to impart human rights education and are popular with the academics as well as with the laymen.

The members of the NHRC and its other functionaries have been much in demand to address various seminars and symposia on different human rights related issues. They have participated in the end number of these events and made maximum use of these platforms for the purpose of generating public awareness about human rights.[29]

A number of major seminars were supported by the NHRC. They were variously organised by non-governmental organisations, universities, the armed forces or State Human Rights Commissions. One such seminar on 'Human Rights and Terrorism and Human Rights Education' was held in Bangalore in August 1996 to commemorate the thirtieth anniversary of the International Covenant on Civil and Political Rights (ICCPR). It was very well attended seminar. The participation of distinguished justices, diplomats, scholars, administrators and human rights activists helped in enhancing the quality of deliberations and recommendations.[30]

Another major international seminar on 'Human Rights Education' was jointly organised with the Canadian Human Rights Commission in February 1996. It was inaugurated by the President of India and attended by the Special Advisor on National Institutions to the UN High-Commissioner for Human Rights and other leading experts both from the grass-roots and top-brass of different organisations.[31]

Another seminar was held in New Delhi in 1999 as a part of the Indo-British Project on Prison Reforms which was undertaken jointly by the NHRC, the British Council, the Bureau of Police Research and Development and PRAJA, an NGO. It focussed on jail management and training in India and the role of the judiciary in the protection of human rights. It also looked into the changing practices in prisons in other parts of the world with a view to reform India's prison management in the context of human rights parameters.[32]

Similarly, the NHRC has also extended its support to several workshops conducted by research institutions, non-governmental organisations or universities in selected place around the country, including Bhopal, Bhubaneshwar, Bombay, Burdwan, Calcutta, Cuttak, Delhi, Gulburga, Indore, Jammu, Kochi, Madras, Madurai, Patna, Rourkela, Tirupathi, Thiruvananthapuram and Varanasi.[33] Besides participating in these workshops, the NHRC also cooperated by sponsoring the visit to India of foreign academics and human rights activists for this purpose.

To enhance the understanding of human rights and promote exchange of ideas at the regional and international level, the NHRC has been supportive of joint collaboration in the matter of workshops on human rights. For instance, the NHRC held a workshop on 'Managing Human Rights Institutions', in Calcutta in June-July 1997 with the joint collaboration of the Commonwealth Secretariat and West Bengal Human Rights Commission, which was attended by the Commonwealth countries of Asia.[34]

The NHRC has also hosted the Second Asia-Pacific Regional Workshop on National Human Rights Institutions in September 1997 which was attended by the members of the Asia-Pacific Forum together with the representatives of the United Nations agencies, programmes and key-NGOs. In addition, the chairpersons of the State Human Rights Commissions in India also participated in the workshop.[35]

The NHRC has encouraged non-governmental organisations in their effort to organise seminars and workshops with the purpose of gaining better understanding of the specific issues relating to human rights such as women, dalits, disabled persons and child-labour, etc. For instance, a National Workshop on 'Human Rights and Social Change' was held in Madras in joint collaboration with the People's Union for Civil Liberties (PUCL) and the Dalit Liberation Education Trust. It constituted a major effort by the NHRC to better its understanding of the special problems facing the Dalits, helping it to find appropriate ways of resolving and redressing these problems.[36]

Thus, it is indicative of the fact that the NHRC is not always content in playing the preacher's role for others, but is also ready to learn from others to promote the cause of human rights.

Publications and Media

To reach out the people in the big way, the NHRC's dependence on press and media is an obvious need. The NHRC makes use of publications and media for the purpose of dissemination of information which helps in creating awareness about human rights. The media also acts as a watch-dog for the protection of human rights. No doubt, the NHRC considers media as its key-ally in the promotion and protection of human rights.[37]

For the purpose of educating public opinion, the NHRC sought the cooperation of the media, both print and electronic, by way of giving regular press-briefings and continuing the practice of periodic meetings with editors / special correspondents of important newspapers and news channels. The interviews of its chairmen appeared in national dailies putting across their viewpoints about the activities of the NHRC. Some of the members of the NHRC have also shared their views and perceptions with media on various aspects of human rights issues.[38]

The growing interaction between the NHRC and the media has resulted in the increased coverage of human rights issues in the media. The NHRC has noted a marked improvement in the coverage in the range and depth of such coverage since 1993 when the NHRC was established.[39]

The electronic media has also been used to highlight human rights issues in the form of documentaries features, discussions and talks, etc., both on the All India Radio and Doordarshan. The NHRC has received the fullest cooperation from these two state-owned media organisations. The NHRC has prepared twelve 'Spots' which are being regularly broadcast by the All India Radio. In addition to these items, 'Human Rights Watch', a half-hourly programme has been started on monthly basis by the All India Radio. It has been regularly broadcasting spotlight and commentaries on human rights issues. On Human Rights Day, a member of the NHRC participated in a 'Phone-in-Programme' broadcasted by the All India Radio, Private Television Networks, too, have been contacting the NHRC for interviews and other information concerning human rights issues and telecasting programmes on these issues.[40]

The growing media visibility of human rights issues and the activities of the NHRC has prompted a number of film makers to take up projects on human rights issues and make use of the cases handled by the NHRC in their footage.[41]

The NHRC attaches a great importance to the role of media in the protection and promotion of human rights and has commended the role played by the Indian media. Media acts as the eyes and ears of the NHRC as it takes *suo motu* action on reports appearing in the media. At the same time, the activities of the NHRC are also open to media.

No doubt, the NHRC depends heavily on print and visual media for the promotion of human rights, but it also brings out its own publications for the purpose of propagation of information regarding the activities of the NHRC and human rights issues with a view to enlighten people about them.

Initially, it made a humble beginning with a monthly *Newsletter,* in October 1994, which was very well received. *The Newsletter,* published in Hindi and English, got an overwhelming response and its ever-growing demand, inside and outside the country, has forced the NHRC to launch it on its website.[42]

The Clippings Information Service of the NHRC is also of keen interest to researchers, students and academics. All news items relating to human rights scanned from twenty newspapers, are clipped and filed in a computerised database, facilitating retrieval of important clippings topic-wise, date-wise and newspaper-wise. The clippings serve as an important source of information to the NHRC for taking *suo motu* action.[43]

The NHRC has also published two booklets in Hindi and English for the purpose of educating people and creating human rights culture in the country. These booklets contain the 'dos and don'ts in respect of arrest and the convention on the rights of the child.[44]

In addition, the NHRC has introduced a scheme of awards on 'Creative Writings on Human Rights in Hindi' to encourage original writings in Hindi on subjects dealing with human rights.[45] Thus, it has tried to involve public in promoting human rights education.

Research Programmes and Projects

Research forms an integral part of the strategy for the promotion of human rights. The NHRC has been entrusted with the responsibility to carry out research on human rights by the statute. In this matter, it has identified the areas that need to be explored for the purpose of suggesting practical solutions to the problems of human rights. These areas included child-labour, problems of mentally ill and their rehabilitation, female-foeticide and female-infanticide, rights of the tribal women, problems of the aged and revising ways and means for creating human rights culture.[46]

Faced with the problem of financial constraints for the purpose of research and technical restraints placed by the Planning Commission, the NHRC decided to use its own budgetary provisions for research and earmarked a sum of rupees 10 lacs for this purpose. A grant of rupees 1.20 lacs was released to the National Institute of Mental Health and Neuro-Sciences (NIMHANS) in Bangalore, for a study on 'Quality Assurance in Mental Health', to be undertaken on behalf of the NHRC. The NHRC has restructured its Research Division, converting it into a Policy, Research, Projects and Programmes Division (PRPP).[47]

The NHRC, in order to effectively perform its duties, tries to rationalise its policy on the basis of research inputs provided by its PRPP Division which identities and takes up a variety of programmes and projects for research. Pursuant to this goal, the NHRC had referred a number of projects to the National Institute for Human Rights Research and Documentation (IHRERD) at the National Law School of India University, Bangalore. The IHRERD is of great assistance to the NHRC in carrying out its statutory obligation to undertake research on human rights with a view to formulate a policy for the protection and promotion of human rights.

The NHRC had entrusted a number of research projects to the IHRERD which included variety of subjects relating to human rights, such as, the study of human rights treaties and other international instruments on human rights for making recommendations regarding their effective implementation; the problems related with the spread of HIV infection and human rights concerns of the HIV infected persons; the question of jurisdiction of Human Rights Courts under Section 30 of the NHRC Statute; the National Police Commission's observations about the misuse of the power of arrest by the police and the collection of statistics, under the pilot project, as to the reasonableness of the exercise of the power of arrest by the police; and sexual abuse of women and children, etc.[48]

The IHRERD had already submitted reports on the following Research Projects referred to it by the NHRC :

- Imminent problems connected with the spread of HIV infection and human rights concerns of privacy and dignity of HIV positive persons.
- The First Optional Protocol to the International Covenant on Civil and Political Rights (ICCPR) and the question of its ratification by the Government of India.
- The Second Optional Protocol to the ICCPR and options before India.
- International Convention on the Protection of the Rights of all Migrant Workers and their Families a plea for India's ratification.
- Convention against Torture and Other Cruel, Inhuman or Degrading Treatment or Punishment : the case for early ratification.
- The question of jurisdiction of human rights Courts under Section 30 of the Protection of Human Rights Act, 1993.
- Right to Speedy Trial, a compendium of guidelines for speedy trial derived from the decisions of the Apex Court of India.
- Eye donation and transplantation of cornea : national and international dimensions.
- Narcotic Drugs and Psychotropic Substances Act : agenda for reform from human rights perspective.
- Group Accident Insurance Scheme for Fish-Workers : an analysis and a proposal.[49]

Besides promoting research studies, the NHRC pays due attention to a variety of programmes and projects on a regular basis. During the discussion on the Programme Agenda on every Friday and also at the meetings of the Full Commission, these programmes and projects are discussed in detail and where necessary relevant recommendations are made. For example, the studies on the three major projects undertaken on behalf of the NHRC, viz, State of the Art Forensic Science : for Better

Criminal Justice, Large Volume Parenterals Towards Zero Defect and Quality Assurance in Mental Health were considered by the NHRC and the recommendations contained in these studies were accepted by the NHRC and forwarded to the concerned authorities in the Centre and the states with a request to do the needful for their effective implementation.

Internship Programme

Acting on the recommendation made by the management consultants, M/s Mckinsey & Co., the NHRC launched a 'Summer Internship Programme' aimed at providing the requisite exposure to the philosophy and culture of human rights to the successive batches of students and also in a measure to augment the personnel resources of the NHRC. The interns are being paid a monthly stipend of Rs 2000 and are selected on the basis of a strong academic background, a positive interest in human rights issues and good communication skills. The Internship programme is meant for the university students, both from India and abroad, with a view to expose them to the works of the commission. The duration of this programme is six weeks and it is inter-disciplinary in nature. This programme has received very good response from the universities and a large number of students apply for it every year.[50]

Apart from the Summer Internship Programme, the NHRC has given short-term placements to the three students from the National Law School of India University, Bangalore during November-December 1999 and five others during the period January-February 2000.[51] Two other university students, one from Bochum University, Germany and the other from the Fletcher School of Law and Diplomacy, Tuft University, USA were also given placements in the commission same year.[52]

The NHRC also received an offer from the Danish Centre for Human Rights to depute one of its Human Rights Officer to work on a research-project on 'The Conditions of Juvenile Homes and Other Institutions / Homes Set-up under Different Statues', which was accepted by it. A very useful report on this project was submitted to the NHRC thereafter.[53]

Training Programme

To promote the culture of human rights, training programmes prove effective tools of behavioural change. The NHRC in collaboration with the British Council and the Bureau of Police Research and Development conducted a two-weeks training programme for prison-officials with the aim of promoting good practices and gender sensitivity in jail-management. The trainees were to serve as a national resource for further training of trainees in India. The training programme was designed to help Indian prison officials learn from the experience of the United Kingdom in areas of prison-management and to help bring about attitudinal and behavioural changes in management practices.[54]

Further, the NHRC constituted a core-group for the purpose of preparing training-material for the staff of the National and State Human Rights Commissions. The Core-Group consisted of representatives from NHRC, the National Commission for women, Punjab and Himachal Pradesh State Human Rights Commissions, Indian Institute of Public Administration, National Institute of Criminology and Forensic Sciences, Prof. Hargopal of the Central University, Hyderabad and Shri Joseph Gathia, Executive-Director, Centre for Concern for Child-Labour. The task before the Core-Group included preparation of the curriculum, training-manual, resource persons, training schedule and the list of the institutions for the training programme.[55] Thus, the NHRC tried to impart better professional skills to the personnel of human rights institutions (HRIs) through various training programmes.

Interaction with External Groups and Organisations

The doors of the NHRC are open to one and all, because it believes in the transparency of its functioning. Moreover, it provides opportunity to interact with various types of people which is important in understanding the ground realities of the problems concerning human rights issues. For these reasons, the NHRC interacts with outside people whether they be Indians or foreigners; whether individuals or organisations; and whether official or non-governmental.

The work of the NHRC has evinced interest both in the diplomats stationed in India and in the political and academic circle abroad. The NHRC has had several occasions for discussions with members of the diplomatic corps stationed in Delhi. Ministers and other leading personalities visiting the country have often called on the NHRC. Eminent parliamentarians, senators and congressmen, jurists, scholars journalists and representatives of international non-governmental organisations, including Amnesty International have visited the NHRC headquarters and exchanged views with its officials.[56]

The NHRC has welcomed to its headquarters several delegations and functionaries of other regional and national human rights institutions and

United Nation as officials as well. A two member delegation comprising the Deputy chairperson and Executive secretary of the South African Human Rights Commission, the Chief commissioner of the Canadian Human Rights Commission, the Chairperson of the Human Rights Commission of Pakistan, the Director-General of UNESCO, an Associate Administrator of UNDP, the Executive Director of UNICEF, and a number of visiting professors, from abroad interacted with the NHRC.[57]

The interaction is always a two-way process. It is not that the NHRC has been approached by the external groups and organisations all the time, but it has also reached out to other external groups and organisations and contributed towards international cooperation for the promotion of human rights. The chairperson of the NHRC has had the honour of serving as the Chair of the International Coordinating Committee of National Institutions for the Promotion and Protection of Human Rights since April 1996. The NHRC was also requested by the United Nations to depute a member of the NHRC or the Secretary-General to participate in the workshops on National Institutions that were organised in Mongolia, Moldova and Jordon where they were considering to establish such institutions. Further, a member of the NHRC participated in the meeting of the Inter-parliamentary Union in Paris. Similarly, the NHRC has also bee sending its officials to various seminars, workshops, training programmes and study tours to make them learn from others experiences and also to share their own experiences with others.[58]

Networking with Non-Governmental Organisations

Indispensability of non-government organisations to the protection and promotion of human rights is a well known fact. That is why, the NHRC is called upon by the statute to encourage the efforts made by the non-governmental organisations in the field of human rights. The NHRC has also recognized the significance of the role of non-governmental organisations in discharging the duties assigned to it under the statute; and it considers non-governmental organisations as its natural allies, sternest critics and indispensable partners.[59]

The NHRC has perceived its relationship with non governmental organisations as both the constructive and critical, and in both senses it is crucial for the protection and promotion of human rights. The constructive relationship of the NHRC with non-government organisations is revealed in the now well established cooperation between the two in respect of the receipt and handling of complaints relating to human rights, and the conduct of seminars and workshops. Also, non-governmental organisations render invaluable contribution in imparting human rights education and training and in spreading human rights awareness. They are of immense help in providing valuable policy-inputs based on their research studies. In their critical role too, they are the eyes and ears of the NHRC.

With a view to supplement its own efforts, the NHRC has drawn on the vast pool of talent and commitment provided by the non-governmental organisations. No field of activity of the NHRC now remains insulated from these organisations whose advice has been sought on ways to make it more effective. The NHRC utilises the services of non-governmental organisations in reaching out to the grass-roots levels and getting their perspective in understanding complex problems affecting dalits, tribals, child-labour, child-prostitutes, women, disabled, migrants and other vulnerable groups. The non-governmental organisations are also involved in various research projects and programmes in association with the NHRC. They also act as the resource bank for various conselling and practical training programmes.

In order to strengthen the cooperation with non-governmental organisations, the NHRC has also extended modest financial support to these organisations in organising various programmes of relevance to human rights, such as, study programme, seminars, workshops and training programme, etc.[60] The NHRC also sponsored representatives of three non-governmental organisations for a three week International Human Rights Training Programme conducted by the Canadian Human Rights Foundation during June-July 1997, together with members of its own staff.[61] Thus, the NHRC considers it important to help strengthen the capacity of non-governmental organisations through the training of their staff.

Convinced of the need and the benefit of working closely with the non-governmental organisations, the NHRC has been working to prepare a directory of all these non-governmental organisations with a view to expand and strengthen the network of these organisations.[62] This will add to systematised working of the NHRC. Furthermore, the NHRC is planning to set-up an 'NGO – Liaison and Service' unit under its Projects and Programme Division for the purpose of creating a database of active and credible NGOs in the human rights field and promote networking amongst them and the NHRC.[63]

From the above, it is evident that the NHRC's commitment to human rights is total. It has given equal attention to the task of promotion of human rights. The enormity of the challenge has strengthened its resolve to work endlessly for the promotion of human rights. It's all inclusive approach has helped it to get the support of various organisations in this task. The systematic and methodical way has simplified the task. Realising the fact that promotion of human rights culture is a long-term approach, the NHRC has adopted multi-pronged strategy to cultivate human rights values through education, campaigning, publicity and training, etc.

References

1. Section 12 (f) (g) (h) (i) and (j), The Protection of Human Rights Act, 1993.
2. Annual Report of the NHRC (1993-94), para 8.2.
3. *Ibid.*, para 8.3.
4. *Ibid.*, paras 8.5-8.6.
5. *Ibid.*, para 8.5.
6. Annual Report of the NHRC (1995-96), paras 6.6-6.7.
7. Memorandum of Action Taken Report on the Annual Report of the NHRC (1995-96), Ministry of Home Affairs, Government of India, paras 6.4-6.7, p. 34.
8. Annual Report of the NHRC (1995-96), para 6.9.
9. Annual Report of the NHRC (1996-97), para 6.6.
10. Annual Report of the NHRC (1995-96), para 6.12.
11. Annual Report of the NHRC (1993-94), para 8.5.
12. Annual Report of the NHRC (1998-99), para 13.5.
13. *Ibid.*, paras 13.7-13.8.
14. *Ibid.*, para 13.12.
15. *Ibid.*, para 2.25.
16. Memorandum of Action Taken Report on the Annual Report of the NHRC (1998-99), Ministry of Home Affairs, Government of India, para XII, pp. 13-14.
17. Annual Report of the NHRC (1997-98), para 11.2 and 11.3.
18. *Ibid.*, para 11.9.
19. Annual Report of the NHRC (1996-97), para 6.11.
20. *Ibid.*, para 6.12.
21. Annual Report of the NHRC (1993-94), para 8.9.

22. Annual Report of the NHRC (1996-97), para 6.13-6.14.
23. Annual Report of the NHRC (1998-99), para 13.14.
24. Annual Report of the NHRC (1994-95), para 6.4.
25. Annual Report of the NHRC (1995-96), para 6.18.
26. Annual Report of the NHRC (1996-97), para 6.15.
27. *Ibid.*, para 6.16.
28. Annual Report of the NHRC (1997-98), para 11.15.
29. Annual Report of the NHRC (1994-95), paras 6.13-6.15.
30. Annual Report of the NHRC (1996-97), para 6.18.
31. Annual Report of the NHRC (1995-96), para 6.19.
32. Annual Report of the NHRC (1999-2000), para 12.16.
33. Annual Report of the NHRC (1995-96), para 6.20.
34. Annual Report of the NHRC (1997-98), para 11.18.
35. *Ibid.*, paras 11.19-11.20.
36. Annual Report of the NHRC (1996-97), para 6.19.
37. Annual Report of the NHRC (1997-98), para 11.29.
38. Annual Report of the NHRC (1996-97), para 6.25.
39. Annual Report of the NHRC (1997-98), para 11.29.
40. Annual Report of the NHRC (1996-97), paras 6.26-6.28.
41. Annual Report of the NHRC (1998-99), para 13.37.
42. *Ibid.*, para 13.34.
43. Annual Report of the NHRC (1999-2000), para 12.29
44. *Ibid.*, para 12.25.
45. *Ibid.*
46. Annual Report of the NHRC (1995-96), para 6.26.
47. Annual Report of the NHRC (1996-97), paras 6.29-6.31.
48. Annual Report of the NHRC (1998-99), para 13.40.
49. Annual Report of the NHRC (1999-2000), para 12.35.
50. Annual Report of the NHRC (1998-99), paras 13.16-13.17.
51. Annual Report of the NHRC (1999-2000), para 12.8
52. *Ibid.*, para 12.10.
53. *Ibid.*, para 12.9.

54. Annual Report of the NHRC (1998-99), para 13.21.
55. Annual Report of the NHRC (1999-2000), para 12.11.
56. For details of these visits, see Annual Reports from 1994-95 to 1999-2000.
57. Annual Report of the NHRC (1997-98), para 15.1.
58. Annual Report of the NHRC (1996-97), paras 10.4-10.5.
59. Annual Report of the NHRC (1998-99), para 14.1.
60. Annual Report of the NHRC (1999-2000), para 13.5.
61. Annual Report of the NHRC (1997-98), para 12.5.
62. *Ibid.*, paras 12.2-12.3.
63. Annual Report of the NHRC (1999-2000), para 13.3.

Chapter VI

Concluding Observations

In today's civilised world, human rights are integral to democratic governance. Building strong human rights institutions at the national level is what in the long-run will ensure that human rights are protected and advanced in a sustained manner. National human rights protection system comprises all those structures and institutions of democratic governance which ensure that all persons enjoy all human rights. National human rights institutions such as India's National Human Rights Commission is merely one of the many other structures and institutions comprising the national human rights protection system.[1] Therefore, any appraisal of the role of NHRC in the protection and promotion of human rights must give due consideration to this fact that the NHRC is not the sole institution responsible for the protection and promotion of human rights in the country.

India's National Human Rights Commission was established at a time when very few such institutions existed in other parts of the world and still fewer of them were Paris Principles compliant institutions. Moreover, the manner in which the NHRC was established also invited a lot of criticism both by the opposition and the non-governmental human rights groups. Doubts were raised about the real intentions behind this move of the government to form 'its own human rights commission.'[2] To some critics, the establishment of the NHRC meant 'succumbing to international pressures'[3] while for others it was merely a 'cosmetic exercise.'[4] No doubt, there was an element of truth in these criticisms, but the establishment of the NHRC and its performance over the years has succeeded in erasing the doubts in the minds of its all critics. Not only this, but it has turned out to be a role-model institution for other NHRIs internationally as it is often asked to act as advisor to those countries who are in the process of establishing such institutions in their own countries.[5]

The Paris Principles are considered as the touchstone to judge the performance of national human rights institutions. Based on the criterion laid down by the Paris Principles, the process of establishing an NHRI is as important as the actual creation of the institution. The process needed to be :

- Consultative, inclusive and transparent;
- Led and supported at the highest level of government; and
- Involve and mobilise all relevant elements of the state and civil society.[6]

The manner in which the NHRC was established, is criticised as being rushed through process, non-inclusive of non-governmental view points and imposing in the form of an ordinance. No doubt, the government was in a great hurry to have a national human rights commission of 'its own' and it was conceived as a defence mechanism to silence the national and international outcry against the sad state of human rights in the country. But this 'ill-conceived' solution offered by the government led to a public debate even if by default. The government move came in for a lot of criticism and the proposed bill was thoroughly dissected at the Parliamentary Standing Committee stage wherein opinions of experts and specialists were sought on the matter. The government learnt its lesson fast and hurried to replace the Bill with an ordinance which was greatly modified in the light of the suggestions made at the Standing Committee. Thus, the NHRC which finally shaped out under the Protection of Human Rights Act, 1993 was quite different from the original version which was initially conceived by the government. It has accommodated the views of human rights community and experiences of NHRIs of other countries as well. That is why, the apprehensions expressed about its 'qualified independence'[7] proved false alarms.

It is true that the charter of the NHRC is not a model charter for NHRIs. It has its own flaws and shortcomings. Yet, the NHRC has 'used' its composition, independence and transparency to achieve some of its objectives for 'better protection' of human rights.[8] The essential components of an effective NHRI are :

- Independence;
- Mandate and powers;
- Accountability and relationship with other institutions, and
- Accessibility.

The effectiveness of the NHRC needs to be judged on the above mentioned counts.

Independence of the NHRC

The independence of a NHRI is understood in relation to its composition, functional autonomy and financial autonomy. The statute of the NHRC provides it with the independence, functional autonomy and broad mandate that are essential to the proper functioning of a national institution based on the principles relating to the status of national institutions (Paris Principles).

In the matter of the composition of the NHRC, broad guidelines of the Paris Principles are accepted in the statute ensuring the independence of the NHRC, such as, the membership possessed with integrity, experience and expertise, consultative procedure of appointment of the members, the terms and service conditions ensuring the independence of the commission.[9] The strict criteria for appointment and dismissal of the members surpasses the requirements of the Paris Principles as the statute renders the commissioners ineligible for appointment under the government, once their term at the NHRC expires. And also, the presence of judges lends prestige to the institution and a degree of solemnity to their recommendations.[10]

However, critics do not fail in pointing out certain drawbacks in the composition of the NHRC. According to them, the composition of the NHRC does not reflect the pluralism and diversity of the society and also does not ensure gender-balance.[11] Another drawback is that the membership of the NHRC is devoid of any representation from the human rights NGOs.[12] Furthermore, one glaring shortcoming is pointed out by the eminent chairperson of the NHRC himself. It relates to the procedure of appointment of the members of the NHRC where the chairperson is not required to be consulted. According to him, 'Since the responsibility for smooth functioning of the NHRC including the making of roster of cases falls on the chairperson, it is necessary that he must be consulted before a person is appointed to the commission and his views given appropriate weightage.'[13]

No doubt, these criticisms are substantive in nature and are meant to enhance the credibility of the NHRC. However, none of these have the effect of jeopardising the independence of the NHRC and at the same time, the performance of the NHRC has not given any reason to complain about the matters concerning pluralistic and gender-sensitive approach. Moreover, the composition of the NHRC has included above concerns indirectly by providing for the ex-officio membership of the commission to the chairpersons of the national commissions on minorities, scheduled castes and scheduled tribes and women.

On the issue of functional autonomy of the NHRC, the chairperson and members are not subordinate to any one in regard to the discharge of their duties. The Act authorises the NHRC to regulate its own procedure of working and appoint its staff and organise the secretariat.[14] The broad range of its functions under the Act, are amongst the widest conferred on any national institution in the world – and have, therefore, served as a possible model for others to consider.[15] There is no appeal against the recommendation of the NHRC. The High Court and the Supreme Court, of course, have rights under the Constitution to issue writs/orders or directions against the state or any authority, including the NHRC.[16]

The functional autonomy of the NHRC is not confined to the statute only. It is reflected in its conduct and actions. Unfazed by the apprehensions expressed by the critics of the commission about the functional autonomy of the NHRC calling it with names like 'toothless tiger', 'post-office', '*Sarkari* body', etc., the NHRC, in the very first case, took *suo motu* action in the tragic incident at Bijbehara in Jammu and Kashmir involving elements of the security forces. The limited mandate, to inquire into the matters relating to armed forces, failed to dissuade the NHRC to persistently pursue the matter with the Government of India.[17] Similarly, in its very first annual report, the NHRC made recommendations to amend the certain provisions of the Protection of Human Right Act, 1993 to better protect and promote human rights. Later, it appointed a high-level advisory committee headed by Justice A.M. Ahmadi to make an in-depth study of the Act which has suggested certain amendments in the various clauses of the Act. The government has yet to make a move in this regard. In the meantime, the NHRC has not waited upon events, it has constantly sought to use and interpret its powers and functions under the Act as expansively and responsibly as it could, keeping in mind its over-arching responsibility to promote and protect human rights in the country and to create a culture in which such rights would be nurtured and respected.[18]

Sometime, the functional autonomy of the NHRC is doubted on the ground that it does not have its own investigation team. It is argued that 'Unless the NHRC has its own investigating machinery, it would remain a lame-duck and that to ask the government agencies to investigate human rights violations is like asking the violator to give judgement on his own misdeed.'[19] Another observation is that the commission is rendered weak by its meager investigative powers and by the lack of an independent investigation team at its disposal.[20]

But, it needs to be emphasised that the investigations carried out by the NHRC are always impartial and fair despite the fact that the investigation team is picked up from the government agencies. The independence of the investigation is assured because the NHRC enjoys the power to select the investigation officers of its own choice and they have to take directions from the NHRC and follow the procedure set by the NHRC. They are accountable to the NHRC. So far, the experience has shown that the investigation division of the NHRC has opted for such personnels who are known for their integrity, professional ability, impeccable qualities of character and human rights sensitivity.

Another important element affecting the independence of the NHRC is the financial autonomy of this institution. As regards the finances of the NHRC, it is authorised to prepare its own budget on the basis of which the Centrel Government formulates the proposal for grant and places the same before the Parliament. The Parliament passes the law providing for due appropriation of grant to the NHRC. The NHRC is free to spend the amount as it deems fit for performing its functions and enjoys financial autonomy vide Section 32 (2). The government cannot play around with the budget of the NHRC after it is passed by the parliament.

Although, the financial autonomy of the NHRC has been assured by the statute; yet sometimes, the bureaucratic and administrative hassles come in the way of its functional and financial autonomy. For example, the NHRC felt constrained to undertake its research activities in the manner that it desired due to trivial objections raised by the Planning Commission which was the funding agency in the particular case.[21] However, the NHRC decided to overcome this hurdle by using its own budgetary provisions.[22] Thus, the NHRC refuses to make any kind of compromise with its functional and financial autonomy.

Mandate and Power

An NHRI should have a broad mandate covering full range of human rights issues and recognising the universality, interdependence, interrelatedness, and indivisibility of human rights. Also, the legislative base of NHRI should confer a power to take such action as is necessary and convenient to enable the institution to discharge its mandate.[23] From this angle, the NHRC has been given a broad mandate covering the full range of human rights issues, but the powers conferred do not commensurate with the tasks assigned.

The restrictive nature of the statutory provisions relating to the powers of the NHRC often create doubts about the capabilities of the commission. Narrowly defined 'human rights', meager investigative powers, particularly in respect to the armed forces, and merely recommendatory powers of the NHRC provide a weak ground for it to stand on. But, the structural weaknesses of the statute have been duly compensated by the firm determination of the NHRC to make the best of the situation.

The NHRC has adopted a positive approach. From the very first year of its existence, it has proposed to make amendments to the Act with a view to remove ambiguities and impediments for the better protection and promotion of human rights. But, its recommendations have been ignored by the government. Meantime, the NHRC has tried to build on such strengths as its statute contains and to construe the other provisions of the statute in ways that are most compatible with the high purposes of the objects and reasons of the Act.

There are several examples where the NHRC has used its imaginative approach to broaden the scope of existing provisions of the Act. For example, the NHRC made it clear that the recommendations of the National and State Human Rights Commissions have to be dealt with by the governments, not as some recommendations amenable to their discretion whether to accept or reject them. Rather, the state governments, under the Protection of Human Rights Act, 1993, are bound, within the time-frame prescribed by Section 18 (5), to forward to the commission their comments 'including the action taken or proposed to be taken thereon.' This obligation has significant relationship to and requires to be read with sub-section 2 of the Section 18, under which the commission has the right, and in appropriate cases the duty, to approach the Supreme Court or the High Courts. The provisions in Section 18 (2) and (5), read together and properly construed, impose 'reporting obligations' on the Centrel and State Governments. It would, indeed, be appropriate for national and state commissions, wherever they consider that the responses of the state governments do not accord with justice and fail to protect and promote human rights, to hold if necessary, public sittings, in which the appropriateness, reasonableness, propriety and the legality of the responses of the state governments would be heard and discussed so as to enable the commissions to decide whether further steps under sub-section (2) of Section 18 would be necessary to be adopted.[24]

Sometimes, the Supreme Court has acted to broaden the scope of the powers of the NHRC under the Act by delegating its own judicial powers, as happened in the case of mass cremation of unidentified dead bodies by Punjab police,[25] where the NHRC acted as a body *sui generis* at the direction of the Supreme Court. As a body *sui generis*, the shackles and limitations under the Act are not attracted to this body as it does not function under the provisions of the 'Act' but under the remit of the Supreme Court.

Thus, the NHRC has shown that statutory limitations cannot have the effect of diminishing its performance. Contrary to it, the NHRC has overcome the hurdles of the statute by its incredible performance and earned the praise of its staunch critics.

Accountability of the Nhrc

Power corrupts and absolute power corrupts absolutely. In democracy, no institution should have absolute powers of function without appropriate checks. The autonomy of an institution is always accompanied by an element of accountability. So is the case with the NHRC. Its functional and financial autonomy is intrinsically linked to its accountability. The statute of the NHRC enjoins upon it the duty to submit an annual report to the Centrel Government and to the state government concerned and may at any time submit special reports on any matter which, in its opinion, is of such urgency or importance that it should not be deferred till submission of the annual report.[26] Further, the Centrel Government and the state government, as the case may be, shall cause the annual and special reports of the commission to be laid before each House of Parliament or the State Legislature respectively, as the case may be, along with a memorandum of action taken or proposed to be taken on the recommendations of the commission and the reasons for non-acceptance of the recommendations, if any.[27] Thus, the statute has provided for a reporting system whereby the NHRC and the government both are made accountable to the Parliament for their actions and activities relating to the mandate of the statute.

Apart from the accountability towards the parliament, the NHRC is also accountable to the public as well. It is for this purpose that the commission must act, and be seen to act at all times, with autonomy and transparency. It is on these two conceptual pillars that the NHRC's work must rest if it to sustain and enhance the trust reposed in it by the nation.[28]. This has been the conceptual approach of the NHRC right from the time of its inception.

The transparency of the NHRC rests both on its statute and on the regulations which govern its procedures. The increase in the number of complaints received by the NHRC led to drastic changes in its procedures for dealing with them. It has been the effort of the NHRC to ensure the speedy and efficient handling of all complaints to the satisfaction of the complainants as much as possible. The NHRC's heightened sense of accountability, particularly public accountability has led it to pay the innovative attention to the entirely new challenges in order to ensure that the most vulnerable do not remain the least protected, the least respected.[29]

The accountability of the NHRC is well reflected in its relations with the non-governmental human rights groups and the judiciary of the country. The NHRC has developed a healthy relationship with the NGOs as it looks upon them as 'the most natural allies and most honest critics.' The close proximity of the NGO's with the NHRC helps in assuring public accountability of the NHRC. Similarly, the symbiotic relationship that the NHRC shares with the Supreme Court ensures the requirement of judicial accountability. Thus, the NHRC's working comprises public, executive, legislative and judicial accountability and autonomy as well.

Accessibility

The measure of an NHRI's effectiveness includes its easy accessibility to all groups and individuals in the society. The NHRI should be geographically and physically accessible by constituents, including people with disabilities. The NHRI's credibility depends on this factor of accessibility which includes efficient complaint handling procedure and wide reach of the NHRC throughout the country through decentralised agencies.[30]

From this point of view, the statute and the rules of procedure governing the functioning of the NHRC ensures that the access to it is open, easy and cheap. The easy accessibility of the NHRC has made people prefer to approach NHRC instead of the judiciary where the process is expensive and cumbersome.[31]

In order to facilitate its accessibility to one and all, the NHRC has been persistently persuading the state governments to establish State Human Rights Commissions at the earliest. Meantime, it is trying to find alternative mechanism for the swift and inexpensive redressal of complaints. The ever growing number of complaints reaching the office of the NHRC is a pointer to the accessibility of the NHRC. To enhance its accessibility, the NHRC interacts with the various government departments / ministries, international organisations, non-governmental organisations and participates in various meets. Thus, the NHRC provides easy and ready access to the individuals and groups as well.

How Much Effective is the NHRC

There are two levels on which the effectiveness of the NHRC needs to be assessed. At the first level, we would like to know, how the government has taken the recommendations and directives of the NHRC? What has been the response of the government to the NHRC? Whether the NHRC is getting desired cooperation from the government or not? The effectiveness of the NHRC at the level of the government is very important in the matter of human rights protection and promotion because the state / government is the main accused of human rights violations. Unless, there is a change of attitude and behaviour in the working of the government functionaries, the purpose of the NHRC gets defeated.

It has been the experience of the NHRC, by and large, that its recommendations, directions and 'guidelines' have been observed without being challenged, though, on occasions, a review has been sought of the commission's decisions. In a limited number of instances, however, the authorities or public-servants held responsible for violation of rights have sought to block the jurisdiction of the commission or challenge its decisions before the superior courts of the country or before other commissions. Generally speaking, it can be said that the Apex Court and the High Courts have invariably upheld the positions taken by the Commission. This had added great strength to the commission. It has also underlined the fact that the NHRC plays a role complementary to that of the superior courts of the country in the defense of human rights and constitutional guarantees, a role that has often been described as symbiotic.

No doubt, general response of the government towards the NHRC's recommendations is quite positive. Apparently, it gives the impression as if the government's commitment to human rights is total and it has full faith in the NHRC. But a closer scrutiny of annual reports of the NHRC and the action taken reports reveals a different fact. The positive response of the government to the recommendations made by the NHRC is restricted to those matters only which have implications for the common people and those which do not affect political interests of the government. In the matters that have lasting impact on the interests of the government, the government response has been either lukewarm or negative. For example, the NHRC has been making repeated recommendations relating to necessary structural changes in the statute, but the government is keeping quiet on this matter for so long.[33] Similarly, with regard to the recommendations concerning the armed forces personnels, the government has openly shown its unwillingness to make desired changes in the procedure of investigation.[34] Also, the persistent calls of the NHRC urging the government to ratify the UN Convention against Torture have yielded no results so far.[35]

Moreover, the government agenda gives a low priority to the NHRC as it shows least concern to its statutory obligation to place the annual reports of the NHRC before the Parliament on time. The time lagged between the submission of the report and placing it before Parliament was more than nine-months in respect of the annual report for the year 1996-97, while it was twelve months for the report of 1997-98 and 13 months for the report of 1998-99.[36]

Further, the government attitude towards the recommendations made by the NHRC is rather casual as is evident from the action taken reports. The NHRC itself has observed that successive action taken reports have been less than clear in respect of whether, recommendations of the commission will be implemented or what the time-frame will be for the implementation of recommendations. Further, when the recommendations pertain to the states, the NHRC expects that the Centrel Government will use its best efforts to secure compliance at the earliest. Too often, however, the action taken reports simply indicate that the recommendations in question falls within the competence of the states and does not indicate what, if anything, will be done thereafter.[37]

The attitude of the Parliament with respect to the annual reports, of the NHRC and the memoranda of action taken reports by the government is quite indifferent. There is hardly any discussion taking place in the parliament on these reports. The whole significance of these annual reports of the NHRC seems to be totally lost on the members of Parliament. They hardly pay any heed to it. This parliamentary apathy is rather unfortunate because the Parliament like the Supreme Court can play a complementary role to the NHRC in promoting the cause of human rights in the country.

From the above an inference may be drawn that the state lacks fervour for the NHRC and its activities. The aspersions cast about the intentions of the government in establishing the NHRC seem true implying that the establishment of the NHRC was a political compulsion for the government which was done to dispel the misgivings of international community with regard to the state of affairs of human rights in the country in order to avoid the stopping of foreign financial aid. They had no genuine concern for human rights.[38]

The effectiveness of the NHRC needs to be assessed on another level also, i.e., at the level of public. It is the people who are the aggrieved party in the matter of human rights violation. It is they whose rights are abused and who are the real victims. Therefore, it is important to know whether the establishment of the NHRC has made any difference to them or not? How effectively their grievances are redressed? Are the steps taken by the NHRC helpful in the protection and promotion of human rights?

The first and foremost effect of the NHRC is seen in the form of increased awareness among the people about human rights. The NHRC has provided a kind of legitimacy to the concept of human rights which was missing earlier. According to one human rights activist, 'The establishment of NHRC has made this difference that there are now some important levels where this concept has been accepted, where there is an understanding of the concept.'[39] Not merely this, they are also aware that now, there is an effective grievance redressal mechanism available to them in the form of NHRC which is cheap, easy to access and quick-responding. This is the effect that the NHRC has made on the people that has resulted in the flood of complaints at its headquarters.[40]

The trust reposed in the NHRC has to be sustained for lasting effect. The prompt disposal of complaints with victim-oriented approach of the NHRC has yielded concrete results. From its inception upto 31st March, 2000, the NHRC has ordered compensation in 598 cases. The total amount of compensation that has been ordered is Rupees 7,67,83,634/-.[41] Besides the compensation, the NHRC's recommendations have led to criminal prosecution and departmental action against a good number of public servants responsible for the violation of human rights. The NHRC has played both the reactive and pro-active role in the protection and promotion of human rights.

Apart from handling the individual complaints, the NHRC deals with diverse and varied problems relating to human rights including the untouched areas such as public health, natural calamity, hunger & starvation, etc. It is also actively engaged with issues relating to systemic reform and good governance including policy choices which are central to the 'better protection' of human rights in the country and to 'matters connected therewith' or 'incidental thereto.'

Moreover, the efforts of NHRC for the promotion of human rights awareness and cultivation of human rights culture are going to have a lasting effect for securing human rights, peace and development. Human Rights education and human rights training programme are helpful in sensitising the people at all levels. The NHRC is receiving complaints from all segments of society from all parts of the country including those affected by terrorism and insurgency. In this respect, the NHRC has played a therapeutical role, holding out the hope of justice and fair-play even to the most deprived and alienated.[42]

NHRC as an Institution of Good Governance

The quality of governance and the promotion of human rights have a deep co-relation. The NHRC is of the view that the promotion and protection of human rights – the expansion of essential freedoms – must be the central purpose of governance. And this can be assured by probity, and honesty, by diligence and a sense of direction that places the concerns of the disadvantaged and vulnerable foremost in the considerations of policy and actions."[43]

With this core-message, the NHRC has repeatedly drawn attention to the need to keep the institutions of governance in good repair and stressed the importance of probity, civility and tolerance as being to sound political conduct and attitudes of those in authority. Therefore, it has been consistently pressing for systemic reforms in police, the custodial justice system and also in the criminal justice system.[44]

The NHRC is itself an institution of good governance, committed to transparency, autonomy, accountability and efficiency in its working. Right from the time of its inception, it has been striving to evolve as an institution of good governance focussing on building necessary infrastructure, formulation of its rules of procedure and setting its priority. To ensure efficiency, quality and credibility, it has streamlined its working and adopted innovations for better management and greater productivity.

Realizing the importance of institution-building for the sustenance of any system, the NHRC has promoted healthy practices and set good precedents, emerging as a self-sustained body rather than being an organisation revolving around individuals. This fact has been admitted by one PUCL official who commented, 'The departure of Mr Justice Ranganath Mishra, may have made some difference in the complexion of the working. May be the present chairperson is not, an activist type which Mr Mishra was. But in the level of activity of the commission, the effectiveness or ineffectiveness, whatever, of the commission, there has been no deterioration because the commission is becoming an institution.'[45]

The NHRC's sense of commitment to institution-building efforts and strengthening the institutions of good governance is punctuated with sense of caution as it points out,

'Institutions of governance, to have a lasting value, need to prove their worth each day. A single major failure can be more calamitous than numerous small successes. And trust in an institution can dissipate as rapidly as it is conferred, should an institution fail to maintain the standards of integrity, efficiency and probity expected of it. The maintenance and sustenance of institutions of governance – and especially of those which are themselves corrective in character – thus becomes of the highest importance, and far more onerous a responsibility than the mere establishing of such institutions.'[46]

For this reason, the NHRC has, while discharging the varied responsibilities entrusted to it by its statue, sought to set in place systems and practices that would bring to its efforts an over-all sense of order, coherence and form and ensure accountability and transparency in its functioning. However, the efforts of the NHRC need the backing of the other organs of the state to have the desired results.

Problems Faced by the NHRC

During the course of its five year journey, the NHRC has come across several problems which have adversely affected the potential of the NHRC in accomplishing the tasks assigned to it. The first and foremost problem faced by the NHRC concerned the unfavourable public-opinion relating to the real nature of the NHRC. The strong biases and prejudices against the NHRC had resulted in a negative-image building about the NHRC even before it came into existence. The NHRC had to fight out this negative image and work for the constructive positive image by establishing its credibility in the eyes of common public.

Another problem surfaced in the form of structural impediments effecting the potential of the NHRC. Although, the NHRC came to realise it from the very start of its functioning and made thorough recommendations for the necessary amendments in the statute, but the government inaction and diffidence in this matter is posing difficulties for the NHRC to fulfill its obligations under the statute.

The continued growth of work-load of the NHRC is also a big problem as it does not get the required work-force to ensure quick and efficient disposal of the work. The shortage of staff and the delay in filling the vacancies adversely affect the credibility of the NHRC. Until such time when the NHRC develops its own cadre, the NHRC has to bear with this problem.

Closely related with the problem of logistical shortages is the problem of financial constraints. The tasks assigned to the NHRC by the statute are quite enormous which demand liberal financial grants. But many times, the NHRC has faced financial crunch resulting in either postponing the project or seeking grants from other sources.

Many times, the NHRC has to face bureaucratic way of functioning in various departments of the government causing unnecessary delays and irritation. Implications of the NHRC's independence are not always acted upon as clearly or swiftly as they should have been in matters that are generally of an administrative nature. This can be extremely tiresome and time-consuming, especially in respect of matters for which overall budgetary provisions already exist. This kind of relationship of the NHRC with the government is also violative of the principles relating to the status of national institutions – the so-called 'Paris Principles.'[47]

Furthermore, the repeated delay in the placing of the NHRC's annual reports before the Parliament and the absence of any substantive debate on these reports indicate political apathy towards the NHRC. Since the NHRC is merely recommendatory body, the government inaction nullifies all the good work done by it. This is a serious problem that the NHRC has come across and it has been trying to impress upon the government need to avoid such delays and to take necessary action on various recommendations contained in these reports.

Besides these problems, the NHRC has also experienced a variety of challenges during the course of first five years of its establishment. The challenges included challenge of credibility, challenge of scale of workload and high expectation, challenge of variety of problems / cases, challenge of good governance and challenge of entrenched attitudes. Undeterred by these challenges, the NHRC has responded positively and innovatively to serve the cause of human rights.[48]

Considering these facts, it is quite clear that without required political will of our leadership, the NHRC alone cannot act as a powerful protector of human rights. Unless our political leadership provides the necessary back-up to the NHRC, no progress can take place in the matter of protection and promotion of human rights. To make the NHRC more than merely a recommendatory body, demands greater participation and representation of non governmental organisations, strengthening and activation of civil society institutions, enhancing economic resources and empowering the NHRC with punitive powers.

Summing up, human rights are essential norms of democratic governance. The growing recognition of the importance of international human rights standards, and their further development, and an appreciation of human rights as interdependent, indivisible and interrelated, are background for the work of national institutions of human rights protection system.

In the context of India, whatever be the circumstances, whatever be the reasons and whatever be the intention of the government with regard to the establishment of the NHRC, but it was definitely a step without precedent. No doubt, its birth evoked a lot skepticism, but its performance earned the goodwill and appreciation from the protagonists and antagonists alike.

Charged with the onerous responsibility to ensure the 'better protection of human rights', the statute has assigned the NHRC a whole range of functions relating to protection and promotion of human rights. Added to it, the NHRC's ever-increasing case-load is incomparable to any other national institution for human rights in the world. Besides meeting the challenge of ever-growing work-load, the NHRC has to establish its credibility as an independent, autonomous, accountable and transparent body capable of efficient working.

The NHRC has undertaken its responsibilities fairly seriously despite the limitations within which it was to function, and in the short period of its five years working it has done commendable work. As an institution set up by the government, manned by personnels drawn from the government, and whose main job was to enquire into the complaints of human rights violations – mostly against the government and public servants – it is really creditable that the NHRC has played its role as the watch-dog of human rights to the hilt, earning a compliment like this from no lesser a person than Ms Patricia Gossman of Human Rights Watch (Asia Division) who said on record, '... that the Human Rights Commission was doing more than many of the human rights groups.'[49]

The NHRC's commitment to human rights is total. Despite the statutory limitations of its mandate, the NHRC has widened the range of its activities and adopted persuasive policy to impress the government of the need to come out clean in the matter of human rights violations including those involving armed forces. As an indirect approach to this problem, the NHRC has resorted to human rights education and training programmes for the armed forces personnels, aimed at bringing attitudinal changes and making them human rights sensitive. At the same time, in the matters demanding immediate intervention by the NHRC, it does not show any slackness. It does not hesitate to approach the court. In the words of its first chairman, 'The NHRC wants to act as a catalyst for those who suffer at the hands of the state.'[50] Similarly, the NHRC does not confine itself to only civil and political rights or rights in the national context only. Its range of activities include even 'third generation' rights as well.

To conclude, one may say that the establishment of the NHRC has helped in improving the human rights situation in India. It has made people aware of human rights and also encouraged them to seek their protection in case of violation. No institution can claim that it has done enough for the cause of human rights and the NHRC is no exception to it. However, the experience of the first five years of its existence has strengthened the trust of the people in this institution of governance, paving the way for further capacity – building of the human rights mechanisms in the country.

References

1. Orest J.W. Nowosad, "The ABC of National Human Rights Institutions", *Journal of the NHRC*, Vol. 5 (New Delhi), 2006, p. 50.
2. A background note of the Home-Ministry as quoted by Mohan Ram, "Placating the West" in *Pioneer* (New Delhi), 4 October, 1993.
3. K.G. Kannabiran, "Why a Human Rights Commission?" *Economic and Political Weekly* (New Delhi), 26 September, 1992, pp. 2092-94.
4. S.P. Sathe, "Towards an Effective Human Rights Commissiosn", *Economic and Political Weekly* (New Delhi), 3 October, 1992, pp. 2155.

5. A delegation from Bangladesh led by its Minister of Law and the Chairperson of the Human Rights Commission of Pakistan held discussions with the NHRC on the composition, powers and functions of National Institutions set up for the promotion and protection of human rights. Annual Report of the NHRC (1996-97), para no. 10.3

   The efforts of the NHRC have not gone without interest to other countries and they have shown keen desire to associate the NHRC with the evolution of National Institutions in other parts of the World. Annual Report of the NHRC (1996-97), para no. 10.6.

6. 'National Human Rights Institutions : Best Practice', Commonwealth Secretariat, London : 2001, p.9.

7. Vijayashri Sripati, "India's National Human Rights Commission : Strength and Weakness" in *National Human Rights Institutions : Articles and Working Papers* (eds.) Birgit Lindsnaes and Others, The Danish Centre for Human Rights : 2000, p. 154.

8. Justice A.S. Anand, "Role of National Human Rights Institutions : Indian Experience", *Journal of the NHRC*, Vol. 4, 2005, p. 62.

9. Sections 3 to 8 of the Act.

10. According to Vijayashri Sripati, the NHRC is primarily a judge-based body with three of its five members being judges. In the six years of its existence, the NHRC has only for the second time come to have a woman judge as a commissioner. See, "India's National Human Rights Commission : Strengths and Weaknesses" in *National Human Rights Institutions : Articles and Working Papers.* Danish Center for Human Rights, 2000, pp. 154-155.

11. Amnesty International's Summary of Submission to the Advisory Committee established to review the provisions of the Protection of Human Rights Act, 1993. *AI Index : ASA20/26/98,* October 1998, p. 17.

12. Mangari Rajendar, "*The Protection of Human Rights Act, 1993 and Relating Laws*" (Hyderabad : 2000), p. 13.

13. A.S. Anand, op. cit., p. 65.

14. Sections 10 and 11 of the Act.

15. Virendra Dayal. "Evolution of the National Human Rights Commission, 1993-2002 : A Decennial Review", *Journal of the NHRC*, Vol. 1, 2002, p. 43.

16. A.S. Anand, op. cit., p. 67.

17. Annual Report of the NHRC (1999-2000), paras no. 3.7-3.8.

18. Annual Report of the NHRC (1998-99), para no. 2.4.

19. Rajindar Sachar, "Human Rights : Investigative powers for the panel," *Hindustan Times* (New Delhi), 27 November, 1992.
20. Vijayashri Sripati, op. cit., p. 160.
21. Annual Report of the NHRC (1996-97), para no. 6.29.
22. *Ibid,* para no. 6.30.
23. Supra no. 6, pp. 18-19.
24. Annual Report of the NHRC (1998-99), paras no. 15.16-15.18.
25. Annual Report of the NHRC (1997-98), pp. 51-53.
26. Section 20 (1) of the Act.
27. Section 20 (2) of the Act.
28. Annual Report of the NHRC (1993-94), para no. 4.1.
29. For the first time since its establishment, the NHRC made the decision to intervene in the wake of a vast natural calamity the super-cyclone in Orissa – in order to make sure that human rights of often marginalized groups were not ignored. Annual Report of the NHRC (1999-2000), para 19.4
30. Supra no. 6, pp. 31-32.
31. A.S. Anand, op.cit. p. 66.
32. Virendra Dayal, op. cit., p. 50.
33. See Memorandum of Action Taken Report on the Annual Report of the NHRC (1994-95), para. 9, p. 3 and also Memorandum of Action Taken Report to the Annual Report (1999-2000), para no. 33, pp. 32-33.
34. Memorandum of Action Taken Report on the Annual Report (1999-2000) of the NHRC, para no. 6, pp. 15-16.
35. *Ibid,* para no. 34, p. 33.
36. Annual Report of the NHRC (1999-2000), Summary of the Report and of the Principal Recommendations, Annexure No. 19, para no. 1, p. 221.
37. *Ibid,* para no. 2, p. 221.
38. Mohan Ram, "Placating the West", *The Pionner* (New Delhi), 4 October 1993.
39. Y.P. Chhibar, "National Human Rights Commission : A View from Peoples' Front", *Human Rights : Fifty Years of India's Independence,* (ed.) K.P. Saksena (New Delhi : 1999), pp. 122-123.
40. In the first six months of its establishment, the NHRC received 496 complaints which went on swelling with each passing year. In 1998-99, it reached 40,724 in number.

41. Annual Report of the NHRC (1999-2000), para 16.9, p. 84.
42. Virendra Dayal, op. cit., p. 51.
43. Annual Report of the NHRC (1998-99), p. 148.
44. *Ibid.*, para no. 2.15.
45. Y.P. Chhibar, op. cit., p. 126.
46. Annual Report of the NHRC (1997-98), para no. 17.6.
47. *Ibid.*, para no. 17.10.
48. Annual Report of the NHRC (1998-99), paras no. 2.2-2.26.
49. Report of symposium on "Kashmir : Resolving Regional Conflict", (Ed.) Robert G. Wirsing, Kartikeya Publications, Meerut, 1996 quoted in "National Human Rights Commission : An Assessment of its Functions" by G.S. Bhargava, unpublished paper presented at a national seminar in New Delhi, November 1997, p. 3.
50. "NHRC Widens its Activites", *The Statesman* (New Delhi), 11th February, 1996.

Chapter VII

Post-Script

The main study is, no doubt, confined to the formative initial five years of the inception of the NHRC. However, it is natural to be curious about its journey so far. Here is an attempt to briefly mention some of the important developments that have occurred affecting the working of the NHRC.

Statutory Reforms

One of the most significant development that has taken place is the amendment of the Protection of Human Rights Act, 1993 by an (Amendment) Act, 2006.[1] This amendment has broaden the meaning of the term 'Human Rights' for the purpose of this Act. Earlier, the term 'Human Rights' was restricted to mean only in the context of the two covenants, namely, International Covenant on Civil and Political Rights (ICCPR) and International Covenant on Economic Social and Cultural Rights (ICESCR). But as per the new amendment, the definition of human rights has been enlarged so as to include not only the two above mentioned covenants, but also 'such other Covenant or Convention adopted by the General Assembly of the United Nations as the Central Government may, by notification specify.'[2] It is important to mention that the NHRC had made repeated recommendations to redefine the term 'Human Rights' to enhance the meaning and scope of the term[3] and finally, in 2006, it has materialised in the amended law.

Yet another change has taken place in the constitution of the NHRC under the above mentioned amendment. Earlier, the composition of the NHRC included 'the Chairperson of the National Commission for Minorities, the National Commission for the Scheduled Castes and Scheduled Tribes and the National Commission for Women 'as the deemed members of the Commission' for the discharge of functions specified in clauses (b) to (j) of section 12.[4] As per the amended law, the composition of the commission includes 'the Chairperson of the National Commission for Minorities, the National Commission for the Scheduled Castes, the National Commission for the Scheduled Tribes and the National Commission for Women' as the deemed members.[5] Consequent to this amendment, the number of deemed members has increased from three to four as now there are two separate commissions for scheduled castes and scheduled tribes.

Another significant change under the amended law relates to the functions and powers of the commission. The power of the NHRC to inquire was earlier limited to '*suo motu* or on a petition presented to it by a victim or any person on his behalf.'[6] This power of the NHRC is now enhanced further as the NHRC is empowered to 'inquire on a direction or order of any court.'[7] Furthermore, the monitoring role of the NHRC has got real boost under the amended law. Because, earlier the power of the NHRC to visit any custodial facility required prior intimation to the state government resulting in missing the actual situation on the spot. But now, the NHRC is empowered to visit jails or other institutions under the control of state governments without the requirement of prior intimation thus enabling surprise visits and empowering the NHRC to study the living conditions of the inmates and make recommendations thereon to the government.[8] The amended law also enlarges the scope of the NHRC that wherever it considers necessary or expedient to do so, it may, by order, transfer any complaint filed or pending before it to the State Human Rights Commission who has jurisdiction to entertain the same.[9] One more amendment relates to the procedure concerning the inquiry into complaints. Under the amended law, Section 18 has been modified as 'steps during and after inquiry'[10] in place of earlier wordings as 'steps after inquiry.' It further grants the NHRC the power to recommend the concerned government or authority 'to make payment of compensation or damages to the complaintant or to the victim or the members of his family as it may consider necessary' in cases where the inquiry confirms the violation of human rights or negligence in the prevention of violation of human rights or abetment thereof by a public servant.[11] Earlier, the NHRC did not have any specific power to recommend for compensation or damages.

The amended law also makes some minor changes with regard to the constitution of State Human Rights Commissions. Earlier the State Human Rights Commission consisted of four members excluding the chairperson.

But as per the amended law, the State Human Rights Commission comprises of only two members excluding the chairperson. Earlier, there were two separate categories under Section 21(2) (b) and (c) which required a serving or retired High Court judge and another member who is or has been a district judge in that State respectively. Now, it provides only for 'one member who is, or has been, a judge of a High Court or district judge in the state with a minimum of seven years experience as district judge.'[12] One more change has been brought about in the composition of the State Human Rights Commission. Earlier, it provided for two members to be appointed from amongst persons having knowledge of, or practical experience in, matters relating to human rights. But now, it has been reduced to one member.[13] There is also a provision made for appointing a common chairperson or member or both for two or more state governments.[14] This change is aimed at facilitating cost-effective functioning of the State Human Rights Commissions especially for the smaller states.

From the above, it becomes amply clear that the Protection of Human Rights (Amendment) Act, 2006 has strengthened the NHRC and helped in facilitating its smooth functioning. It has included the various recommendations made by the NHRC emanating from its years of experience to make it more effective in protecting and promoting human rights in India.

Administrative Reforms

Apart from these statutory reforms, the administrative set-up of the NHRC too has undergone a modernisation process. The NHRC has a secretariat headed by the Secretary-General. Earlier, it comprised the administrative division, the policy research, projects and programme division, the law division, the investigation division and the information and public relations units besides the library and the computer cell. In September 2003, a new division has been created to disseminate information and focus attention on sensitising various agencies and sections of the civil society by conducting human rights training programmes. This division is named as the Training Division. The division is headed by a chief coordinator who is a joint secretary rank officer. The chief coordinator is assisted by a senior research officer and other secretarial staff.[15] It imparts diverse training on various human rights issues in collaboration with national level institutes, state-level institutes, law universities and NGOs of repute working in the field of human rights. The activities of the training division of the NHRC have expanded manifold since its inception and it is doing a great job in cultivating the culture of human rights and promoting human rights education.

The working of the existing divisions too has been streamlined to impart efficiency, accountability and transparency in the functioning of the NHRC. The Law division deals with the receipt and disposal of human rights complaints. Earlier, this division was also entrusted with the job of imparting training to the NHRC staff as well as the outside departments. Now, with the establishment of separate training division, the law division is fully devoted to complaint handling job which is quite enormous in itself. The division has set up a Rapid Action Cell to attend to complaints that require immediate attention and action.[16]

Similarly, the Information and Public Relations Unit works to disseminate information relating to the activities of the NHRC through the print and electronic media as well as to provide feedback to the NHRC on media reports relating to human rights issues. This unit is also responsible for the website besides the various publications of the NHRC. A Public Information Officer has also been appointed for the purpose of facilitating information under the Right to Information Act, 2005 and the Joint-Secretary (Personnel and Administration) in the NHRC as the Appellate Authority.[17]

In 1994, the library of the NHRC was primarily established for research and reference purposes. Over the years, it has developed into a full-fledged Documentation Centre equipped with computer and internet facilities. It now offers the complete database of books, documents and articles on the internet and intranet. It also has SCC (Supreme Court Case) online and Library Management System Software Package (*e-granthalaya*). An Online Public Access Catalogue (OPAC) has been specially developed to facilitate quick availability and location of any book available in the library. The NHRC is an institutional member of the British Council Library and DELNET (Developing Library Network) which promotes resource sharing among the libraries.[18]

The workload of the NHRC is constantly increasing and its set-up is expanding accordingly. In 1993, it started with a minimal staff of 44 persons which increased to 282 in 1998. Today, it has a sanctioned strength of 343 workers.[19] The NHRC has adopted modern technology to make its working more efficient. The NHRC with the assistance of the National Informatics Centre (NIC) has developed a user-friendly package for monitoring the status of complaints (COMMONS) which has been further upgraded to Computerised Information Management System

(CIMS) which is now adopted by both States Human Rights Commissions (SHRCs) and National Human Rights Institutions (NHRIs) across the globe.[20]

Right from the time of its inception, the NHRC was aware of the need to follow-up at the field level on the recommendations and directions made by it together with the need for stronger linkages with governmental and non-governmental authorities and others. For this purpose, it instituted a system of special rapparteurs to assist it in the discharge of its more demanding and sensitive responsibilities. These special rapporteurs, chosen from amongst persons of highest repute, unimpeachable integrity and a pronounced commitment to human rights have been of immense help to the commission. They constitute a group, outside the formal administrative structures of the commission and act as the eyes and ears of the commission, to follow up on the endeavours of the commission at the highest levels and with its full authority, and to undertake such special studies and other assignments as may be requested of them from time to time.[21] These special rapporteurs deal with specific issues relating to human rights such as custodial justice, bonded-labour, child-labour and disability, etc., or a zone comprising a group of States to look into human rights concerns and violations.[22]

Another mechanism adopted by the NHRC to enhance its functioning is taking advice of the experts on complex technical issues by constituting core groups of exports on selected subjects. Currently, there are about ten such core/expert Groups working on subjects like health, mental health, disability, NGOs, legal issues, right to food, emergency medical care, refugees, silicosis & unsafe drugs and medical devices, etc.[23]

Quantum of Work-load of the NHRC

There is no doubt that the quantum of workload of the NHRC is constantly increasing with each passing year. In the first six months of its inception, the NHRC received a total of 496 complaints, out of which 274 complaints were rejected and 174 complaints were inquired into with 48 matters finally disposed off with necessary directions.[24] In the year 2009-2010, the NHRC had a total of 1,00,167 cases for examination. These figures include cases that were brought forward from previous years as well as fresh cases registered during the said period. It disposed off 85,587 cases. These figures include 5,929 cases which were transferred by the NHRC to the State Human Rights Commissions (SHRCs) in accordance with the provisions of the Protection of Human Rights Act.[25]

Despite the ever-increasing number of complaints received by the NHRC, the working of the NHRC is better streamlined today. The status of complaints, disposal of complaints and the recommendations made with regard to each of these complaints together with the compliance status of these recommendations is a pointer to the efficient, transparent and prompt working style of the commission. Initially, the NHRC felt restraints to make recommendations for the payment of compensation or damages to the complaintant or to the victim or the members of his family. But now under the amended Act, the NHRC has been empowered to recommend for the payment of compensation or damages to the victim of human rights violation. This has, no doubt, enhanced the effectiveness of the NHRC in taking actions against the human rights violations. It cannot be accused now of being a toothless body. In the year 2009-2010, the NHRC recommended a total amount of Rs 6,29,33,000 as payment of monetary relief / compensation to the victims / next of kin of the deceased in 398 cases. Compliance reports were received in 132 cases and a total amount of Rs 1,98,83,000 was paid to the victims / next of kin of the deceased.[26]

As per the guidelines issued by the NHRC, every death in police and judicial custody is to be reported to the NHRC for its scrutiny irrespective of such death being natural or otherwise. This has resulted in the maximum number of complaints / intimation under the single category, i.e. custodial deaths. Similarly, the state of Uttar Pradesh continues to be the largest contributor of complaints for the NHRC. It accounts for 62% of the total complaints received by the NHRC. It points out that the establishment of State Human Rights Commission has so far not brought out any significant reduction in the number of complaints being received by the NHRC as more than 85% of the complaints received were from the states having their own human rights commissions.[27] The reason behind this trend may be that State Human Rights Commissions are not as active as the NHRC and also, that the State Human Rights Commissions have not earned the trust of the people.

The NHRC has adopted a pro-active role with regard to the promotion of human rights by spreading human rights literacy, sensitising the common man and government functionaries and providing training and technical assistance to various institutions and organisations. It also acts as the facilitator for assessment and enforcement of human rights programme in selected districts of India. It has also taken initiative on the issues of food security by deliberating upon the question of providing legal remedy at affordable cost and simple mechanism; enforcement of right to food; regulation of private sectors; monitoring the implementation of right to food at micro and macro levels; defining the standards of food security; and research and resource support for addressing the issue of right to food. Similarly, it is actively engaged in resolving health issues such as the shortage of doctors in rural areas; illegal medical practices of doctors having fake certificates / degrees, adverse effects of pesticides on the health of common man, occupational diseases such as Silicosis affecting labourers, and problems concerning mental health. Considering right to health as a human right, the NHRC is constantly monitoring the health policies of the government, working of mental health hospitals, health care facilities in rural and tribal areas and also to suggest for affordable medical care in general.[28]

Another function performed by the NHRC is to review domestic legislations and international conventions. It held consultations with stakeholders on the Prevention of Torture Bill, 2010 which sought to provide punishment for torture inflicted by public servants or any person who inflicts torture with the consent or acquiescence of any public servant. This bill is an enabling legislation to ratify the UN Convention against Torture and Other Cruel, Inhuman and Degrading Treatment or Punishment. The NHRC has also advocated to the Government of India to reconsider the issue of accession to the 1977 Protocols additional to Geneva Conventions of 1949 relating to new rules on international armed conflicts and humanitarian law on non-international armed conflicts and Optional Protocol to the UN Convention on the Rights of Persons with Disabilities.[29]

The pro-active role of the NHRC is further reflected in its broad reach training programmes, specially after the establishment of separate training division under the secretariat. These programmes are in the form of internship, summer-training in universities / institutes, training programme for Indian Foreign Service probationers, in-house training for new inductees (officers and staff) in the commission since April 2007, workshops, and online training programme on human rights for police personnels. Besides these training programmes, the NHRC supports conferences, seminars, symposia and lectures to raise awareness about human rights.

In its endeavour to better protect human rights, the NHRC holds annual meetings since 2001 with the chief secretaries and directors general of police to overcome the geographical barrier of distances and to emphasize the importance of the need for quick and expeditious action from the state governments on references made by the NHRC, to resolve the difficulties, if any, faced by the states in complying with the directions, etc. Similarly, the NHRC has also initiated the process of holding annual meetings with the State Human Rights Commissions with a view to expand the scope of coordination with the State Human Rights Commissions, identify possible areas of joint partnerships for the purpose of dealing effectively with the issues of human rights facing the country.

Besides the annual meetings, the NHRC regularly holds periodic meetings on issues, with the government officials, both at the state level as well as at the Centre. The purpose of these periodic meetings is to monitor regularly the progress or compliance of the directions made by the Commission.[30]

The NHRC carries out the task of promotion and protection of human rights in association with credible non-government organisations and civil society organisations and treats them as the most important allies and most honest critics. Together with the special rapporteurs appointed by the commission, the NGOs have provided a 'multiplier effect' to the efforts of the NHRC, giving to it a vast infusion of high ability and public support. To facilitate its interaction with the NGOs and civil society organisations, it has formed a core group of NGOs comprising leading representatives of NGOs and civil society organisations actively engaged with human rights issues. This core group meets half-yearly to apprise the activities undertaken by the NHRC and to promote collaboration between the NHRC and the NGOs for the purpose of furthering the protection and promotion of human rights.[31]

The symbiotic relationship between the NHRC and the judiciary has further strengthened the efforts made by these instiutitons for the protection and promotion of human rights. The NHRC has approached the courts in several cases to protect human rights of the vulnerable people including in pending cases. One such case is 'Best Bakery Case'. Likewise, the Supreme Court reposing confidence in the NHRC in number of cases, which were under its consideration, remitted them to the commission. Some of the important matters remitted by the Supreme Court to the NHRC include starvation deaths in Orissa, monitoring of programmes to end bonded and child-labour, the 'mass-cremation' of persons in certain districts of Punjab, the proper management of institutions of the mentally challenged in Ranchi, Gwalior and Agra and also the Protective Home for women in Agra. The latest in this series is the Salva Judum.[32]

The NHRC is not confined to the territorial boundaries of the country. It is actively engaged in interaction with international bodies and foreign countries as well. Numerous foreign delegations visit the NHRC throughout the year. Apart from these visits to the commission, the NHRC plays an active role internationally in two groupings, namely, Asia-Pacific Forum of National Human Rights Institutions and International Coordinating Committee of National Human Rights Institutions for the Protection and Promotion of Human Rights.[33] Furthermore, the NHRC actively coordinates with the Government of India and plays a key role in the preparation of India Country Paper for submission to the UN High Commissioner for Human Rights for Universal Periodic Review, besides submitting separate brief paper on India on behalf of the commission. The NHRC also routinely participates in conferences, seminars, workshops abroad and exchange visits abroad.[34]

To conclude, one may say that the NHRC's commitment to its mandate is truly sincere and serious. Right from the time of its inception, it has been constantly and steadfastly trying to make improvements in its working with a view to ensure the best protection and promotion of human rights. It's innovative approach, progressive attitude and use of modern technology has ensured efficiency in its working.

The task assigned to the NHRC is greatly challenging one. The independent and impartial functioning of the NHRC is critical to succeed. To work in a fair, just, equitable and sensible manner, the NHRC has found able support from the judiciary and the non-governmental sectors, too. Its credibility is enhanced by the trust reposed by the victims of human rights violations who are approaching it in ever-increasing number every year with their complaints confident of getting justice at last. This is no mean achievement.

The NHRC has emerged as a role-model of national human rights institution for other countries. It has been described as one of the best in the world by Mary Robinson, former United Nations High Commissioner for Human Rights.[35] Yet, it is conscious of the difficulties with which it has to contend. It is an ongoing journey full of unknown challenges demanding relentless commitment to the cause of protection and promotion of human rights from the NHRC.

References

1. The Protection Human Rights (Amendment) Act, 2006; No. 43 of 2006.
2. Section 2 (1) (f) of the above Act.

3. Annual Report of the NHRC (1993-94), para 13.3, p. 34. These specific recommendations were repeated in the second and third annual reports of the NHRC as well.
4. Section 3 (3), The Protection of Human Rights Act, 1993.
5. Section 3 (3), Act of 2006.
6. Section 12 (a) of the Act of 2006.
7. Section 12 (a) of the Act of 2006.
8. Section 12 (c) of the Act of 2006.
9. Section 13 (6) of the Act of 2006.
10. Section 18 of the Act of 2006.
11. Section 18 (a) (i) of the Act of 2006.
12. Section 21 (2) (b) of the Act of 2006.
13. Section 21 (2) (c) of the Act of 2006.
14. Section 21 (6) of the Act of 2006.
15. Achievements of NHRC, Vol. I, (1993-2006), (New Delhi: 2012), p. 4.
16. Annual Report of the NHRC (2009-2010), p.11.
17. Supra no.15, p. 3.
18. Supra no.16, paras 13.6-13.9.
19. Supra no. 15, p.7.
20. *Ibid*., p. 8.
21. *Ibid*., p. 4.
22. Supra no. 16, p. 11.
23. *Ibid*., pp. 11-12.
24. Supra no. 3, para 4.1.
25. Supra no. 16, para 4.2.
26. *Ibid*., para 4.404, p.125.
27. *Ibid*., para 4.5.
28. Achievements of NHRC, Vol. II, (2007-2011), (New Delhi : 2012), pp. 73-78.
29. *Ibid*., p. 105.
30. Supra no. 15, pp. 157-159.
31. Supra no. 16, pp. 111-112.

32. Supra no. 28, pp. 91-93.
33. Supra no. 15, pp. 153-155.
34. Supra no. 28, pp. 113-120.
35. *Ibid.*, p. ix.

Bibliography

Primary Sources

Amnesty International Reports :

- Submission to the Advisory Committee established to review provisions of the Protection of Human Rights Act, 1993; (AI Index : ASA 20/26/98) October 1998.
- The Draft Optional Protocol to the Convention Against Torture : Developing an Effective Tool to Prevent Torture, (AI Index : IOR 51/10/96) July 1996,

Government of India's Documents :

- Annual Report (1993-94), Ministry of External Affairs, Government of India, New Delhi.
- Memorandum of Action Taken on the Annual Reports (1993-2000) of the National Human Rights Commission, Ministry of Home Affairs, Government of India, New Delhi.

Nhrc's Documents :

- A Guide to the Protection of Human Rights Act 1993, NHRC, New Delhi.
- Annual Reports of the NHRC, 1993-2000, New Delhi
- Human Rights News Letters (Monthly) Published by NHRC, New Delhi.

Parliamentary Debates :

- Lok Sabha Debates, Vol. XXVI, Nos. 1-5, 7 December, 1993, New Delhi

- Lok Sabha Debates, Vol. XXVII, Nos. 10-12, 14 December 1993, New Delhi
- Rajya Sabha Debates, Vol. 162, Nos. 16-20, 16 March 1992, New Delhi
- Text of Draft Bill on Human Rights Commission Bill No. 65 of 1993, As Introduced in Lok Sabha, New Delhi, May 1993.

Un Documents :

- *Basic Facts About the United Nations*, Published by United Nations, Deptt. of Public Information, New Delhi, 1995.
- Effective Functioning of Human Rights Mechanisms : *National Institutions and Regional Arrangements*, Report of the Secretary-General, doc. F/CN.4/2005.
- National Human Rights Institutions : *Background and Overview, Professional Training Series No. 4*, Centre for Human Rights, United Nations, (New York and Geneva : 1995).
- National Human Rights Institutions, Best Practice, Common Wealth Secretariat, Legal and Constitutional Affairs Division, Mart borough House, Pall Mall, London, 2001.
- Strengthening of the United Nations : *An Agenda for further Change*. Report of the Secretary-General, doc. A/57/387. UN Human Rights Centre, New York, 2000.
- Vienna Declaration and Programme of Action. Centre for Human Rights, Geneva, 1993.
- *United Nations Action in the Field of Human Rights*, United Nations : New York, Geneva, 1994.

Secondary Sources

Books

- Agarwal, H.O., *Implementation of Human Rights Covenants with Special Reference to India*, Kitab Mahal, Allahabad, 1983.
- Agarwal, H.O., *International Law of Human Rights*, Central Law Publication, Allahabad, 1974.
- Agarwal, R.S., *Human Rights in the Modern World*, Chetana Publication, New Delhi, 1995.
- Basu, D.D., *Human Rights in Constitutional Law*, Prentice Hall of India Pvt. Ltd., New Delhi, 1994.

- Baxi, Upendra (ed.), *The Right to be Human*, Lancer International, New Delhi, 1987.
- Batra, T.S., *Human Rights : A Critique*, Metropolitan Books, New Delhi, 1979.
- Bajwa, G.S., *Human Rights in India : Implementation and Violation*, Anmol Publication, New Delhi, 1995.
- Campbell Tom, et.al. (eds.), *Human Rights from Rhetoric to Reality*, New York, 1986.
- Cranston, Maurice, *What are Human Rights?* Bodley Head, London, 1973.
- Donnelly, Jack, *The Concept of Human Rights*, Croom Helm, London and Sydney, 1985.
- Dowrick, F.E. (ed.) *Human Rights : Problems, Perspectives and Texts,* Aldershot, Gower, 1984.
- Diwan Paras and Diwan Peeyushi (eds.) *Human Rights and th Law : Universal and Indian,* Deep and Deep Publication, New Delhi, 1998.
- Desai, A.R., *Violation of Democratic Rights in India*, Popular Prakashan, Bombay, 1986.
- Forsythe, David P. (ed.) *Human Rights in International Relation*, Cambridge University Press, Cambridge, 2000.
- Hingurani, R.C., *Human Rights in India*, Oxford and IBH Publishing Co., New Delhi, 1985.
- Iyer, V.R. Krishna, *Human Rights and Inhuman Wrongs,* D.K. Publishers and Distributors, New Delhi, 1990.
- Iyer, V.R. Krishna, *The Dialectics and Dynamics of Human Rights in India: Yesterday, Today and Tomorrow,* Eastern Law House Pvt. Ltd., New Delhi, 1999.
- Iyer, V.R. Krishna, *Human Rights and the Law*, Vedal Wadhwa, (Indore), 1984.
- Joshi, Navin Chandra, *Democracy and Human Rights Values : Essays in Honour Shri V.M. Tarkunde,* Sterling, New Delhi, 1979.
- Joyce, James Avery, *Human Rights Basic Documents,* Macmillan Press Ltd., London.
- Jha, R.C. *Resurrecting Human Rights in India*, Sheriden Book Company, New Delhi, 1995.
- Jayapalan, N. (ed.) *Human Rights : Problems and Prospects*, Atlantic Publication, New Delhi, 2000.

- Kashyap, Subhash C. (ed.), *Human Rights and Parliament*, Metropolitan Publication, New Delhi, 1978.
- Kazmi, Fareed, *Human Rights : Myth and Reality*, International Publication House, New Delhi, 1987.
- Kothari, Smitu, Harsh Sethi (eds.), *Rethinking Human Rights : Challenges for Theory and Action*, New Horizon Press, New Delhi, 1989.
- Kothari, Rajni, *State Against Democracy in Search of Humane Governance,* Ajanta Books, Delhi, 1988.
- Lobo, George, *Human Rights in Indian Situation,* Justice Peace Commission, New Delhi, 1991.
- Lindsnaes, Birgit, and Others, *National Human Rights Institutions : Articles and Working Papers*, Danish Centre for Human Rights, Copenhagen, 2000.
- Macfarlance, L.J., *The Theory and Practice of Human Rights*, Maurice Temple Smith, London, 1985.
- Mishra, Pramod (ed.) *Human Rights in South Asia*, Kalpaz Publications, Delhi, 2000.
- Palai, Arun Kumar, *National Human Rights Commission of India : Formation, Functioning and Future Prospects,* Khama Publication, New Delhi, 1998.
- Pal, R.M., Somen, Chakrabarty (eds.), *Human Rights Education in India,* India Social Institute, New Delhi, 2000.
- Rajendra, Mangari, *The Protection of Human Rights Act 1993 and Relating Laws,* Law Book Agency, Hyderabad, 2000.
- Robertson, A.H., *Human Rights in the World,* Manchester University Press, Manchester, 1982.
- Robertson, A.H., *Human Rights in Europe (2nd ed.)*, Manchester University Press, Manchester, 1977.
- Saksena, K.P. (ed.), *Human Rights : Perspectives and Challenges*, Lancer Books, New Delhi, 1994.
- Saksena, K.P., *Teaching Human Rights : A Manual for Adult Education*, Lancer Books, New Delhi, 1996.
- Saksena, K.P. (ed.), *Human Rights : Fifty Years of India's Independence*, Gyan Publication House, New Delhi, 1999.
- Schechter, Michael, *United Nations Sponsored World Conferences : Focus on Impact and Follow up,* United Nations University Press, Tokyo, New York, Paris, 2001.

- Subbian, A., *Human Rights Complaints Systems : International and Regional,* Deep and Deep Publication Pvt. Ltd., New Delhi, 2003.
- Salmi, Jamil, *Violence and Democratic Society : New Approach to Human Rights,* Zed Books, London, 1993.
- Selby, David, *Human Rights,* Cambridge University Press, Cambridge, 1987.
- Singh, Gurubax, *A Commentary on the Protection of Human Rights Act, 1993*, Dominion Law Depot, Jaipur, 1996.
- Shah, C.G., *Assault on Democratic Rights in Contemporary India,* Memorial Trust Publication, Bombay, 1985.
- Vincent, R.J., *Human Rights and International Relation,* Cambridge University Press, New York, 1986.

Journals and Periodicals

- Contemporary South Asia, New Delhi
- Economic and Political Weekly, New Delhi
- Indian Journal of Public Administration, New Delhi
- Indian Journal of Political Science.
- Indian Journal of International Law, New Delhi
- International Studies, New Delhi
- Journal of the Institute of Human Rights, Nagpur
- Journal of International and Comparative Law Quarterly.
- Journal of NHRC, New Delhi
- Journal of Social Action, New Delhi
- Journal of Parliamentary Information, New Delhi
- Link, New Delhi
- Mainstream, New Delhi
- Seminar, New Delhi
- Sikh Review, Ludhiana
- The Administrator, New Delhi

News Papers

- The Asian Age, New Delhi
- The Decan Herald, Bangalore

- The Hindustan Times, New Delhi
- The Hindu, Madras
- The Indian Express, New Delhi
- The News Times, Hyderabad
- The National Herald, New Delhi
- The Observer, New Delhi
- The Organizer, New Delhi
- The Patriot, New Delhi
- The Pioneer, New Delhi
- The Sunday Observer, Bombay
- The Sunday Observer, New Delhi
- The Statesman, Calcutta
- The Statesman, New Delhi
- The Telegraph, Calcutta
- The Tribune, Chandigarh

Index

D

E

I